A
STRAIGHTFORWARD
GUIDE
TO
THE PROCESS OF
CONVEYANCING

FRANCES JAMES

Straightforward Guides
www.straightforwardco.co.uk

Straightforward Guides

© Straightforward Publishing 2013

ISBN 978-1-84716-394-3

Printed in Great Britain by Grosvenor Group Ltd London EC2A 3HB

Cover design by Straightforward Graphics

Printed in England by

This book was accurate at the time of going to press. The information within reflects the nature of the publication. The author and publisher cannot be held liable for any errors and omissions in the book that may cause others to incur loss.

The book has been written on the strict understanding that it is a guide to the process of conveyancing and should not be used to replace a professional conveyancer.

Contents

Index

Appendix

1. Sample conveyancing costs when using a licensed conveyancer

2. Standard letters used in conveyancing

3. Standard forms used in basic conveyancing

****

INTRODUCTION

This book is not a substitute for a qualified professional and is not presented as such. The information contained within is for use as guidance and at all times the advice of professionals should be sought, as only the extremely confident and experienced lay person, or actual practitioner can buy or sell property alone.

Usually, when buying or selling residential property, solicitors or licensed conveyancers are normally used in order to ensure that the transaction proceeds smoothly. Both are regulated professionals whose governing bodies require that they be insured and properly regulated. Licensed conveyancers are regulated by the Council of Licensed Conveyancers, solicitors by the Solicitors regulation Authority or Law Society. Both carry out the process of buying and selling property in a similar way. There are several legal differences between the professions. Conveyancers are allowed to represent both buyer and seller, whereas solicitors generally don't because of conflict of interest. Similarly, licensed conveyancers need not tell their client if they have received a commission from a marketing or referral agency, whereas solicitors must disclose such commissions. In general, licensed conveyancers may be more suited to a lower value or uncomplicated sale-and it will be much cheaper. If the sale is complex and expensive then a solicitor will be better suited.

However, the actual processes of conveyancing are usually a mystery to both buyer and seller who are not privy to the procedures. The aim of this brief but concise book is to throw some light on the basic processes, thus ensuring that those who are involved at least have some understanding of what is happening and can question those acting for them at any given point. The book should be read in conjunction with "A Straightforward Guide to Buying and Selling Property" which deals with the more general aspects such as the involvement of estate agents.

Although it is safe to say that the average basic conveyance of a leasehold flat or freehold house is relatively simple and unproblematic, there are still fundamental ground rules which one must observe.

When purchasing a leasehold flat for example, particularly in a multi-occupied block, the lease has to be very closely scrutinised and all the covenants in the lease understood. Leases can be unintelligible documents, couched in redundant language, badly laid out and misleading at the best of times.

Leases contain landlord and tenants covenants, which impose rights and obligations on the respective parties, particularly in relation to repairing obligations and service charge and ground rent payments. Other covenants may impose an onerous burden on the leaseholder and quite often only an experienced eye can pick this up.

Likewise, the freehold transfer document may contain obligations, which can only be picked up or understood, by an experienced eye.

Therefore, even if you decide to carry out conveyancing yourself you should always get a sound second opinion concerning the lease or freehold document.

In addition, as we will see later, there are two forms of conveyancing in existence, registered and unregistered. The former means that the ownership of land and all that entails, including extent of ownership, is registered at the Land Registry. The very fact of registration ensures that legal title can be verified. Unregistered land has to be proven through production of deeds, which can be time consuming and problematic. Land Registration has been compulsory in the United Kingdom for a while now, but it is still a fact that a fairly significant amount of all property is unregistered.

This book details the processes of conveyancing as it affects both registered and unregistered land. It then goes on to deal with the advanced stages of conveyancing as it affects unregistered land and also the process of conveying registered land.

Following the conclusion, there is a glossary of terms and a list of useful addresses. There is an appendix, which outlines Land Registry forms currently in use for conveyancing property.

Finally this book cannot guarantee that you will be in a position to convey property without expert help, precisely because it is a guide to conveyancing. However, it should enlighten you as to the processes.

1

CONVEYANCING IN CONTEXT

Conveyancing, or the practice of conveyancing, is about how to transfer the ownership of land and property from one person or organisation to another. Land and property can include freehold property, leasehold property (residential) or can include business leases.

It is principally the conveyance of residential property that this book is concerned with.

Essentially, the process of conveyancing lays down clear procedures for the conveyancer and also sets out each party's position during the sale or acquisition.

Before understanding the process of conveyancing, however, it is essential to understand something about the legal forms of ownership of property.

Forms of legal ownership of property

There are two main forms of legal ownership of property in England and Wales If you are about to embark on the sale or acquisition of a house or flat (or business) then you will be dealing in the main with either freehold or leasehold property.

It is very rare indeed to find other forms of ownership, although, with the advent of the Commonhold and Leasehold Reform Act 2002, which became law in May 2002, the government introduced a form of ownership called 'common hold' that in essence, creates the freehold ownership of flats, with common responsibility for communal areas.

Freehold property

In general, if you own the freehold of a house or a piece of land, then you will be the outright owner with no fixed period of time and no one else to answer to (with the exception of statutory authorities).

There may be registered restrictions on title, which we will be discussing later. The property will probably be subject to a mortgage so the only other overriding interest will be that of the bank or the building society. The responsibility for repairs, maintenance and general upkeep will be the freeholders. The law can intervene if certain standards are not maintained.

The deed to your house will be known as the "freehold transfer document" which will contain any rights and obligations. Usually, the transfer document will list any "encumbrances" (restrictions) on the use of the land, such as rights of way of other parties, sales restrictions etc. The deeds to your home are the most important documentation. As we will see later, without deeds and historical data, such as the proof of title, it can be rather complicated selling property. This is why the system of land registration in use in this country has greatly simplified property transactions.

Any person owning freehold property is free to create another interest in land, such as a lease or a weekly or monthly tenancy, subject to any restrictions the transfer may contain.

Leasehold property

If a person lives in a property owned by someone else and has an agreement for a period of time, usually a long period, over 21 years and up to 99 years or 125 years, and in some cases 999 years, then they are a leaseholder. The conveyancing of leasehold property is potentially, far more problematic than freehold property, particularly when the flat is in a block with a number of units.

The lease is a contract between landlord and tenant which lays down the rights and obligations of both parties and should be read thoroughly by both the leaseholder and, in particular, the conveyancer. Once signed then the purchaser is bound by all the clauses in the contract.

It is worth looking at the nature of a lease before discussing the rather more complex process of conveyancing. Again, it has to be stated that it is of the utmost importance that both the purchaser and the vendor understand the nature of a lease.

The lease
Preamble
The start of a lease is called the preamble. This defines the landlord and purchaser and also the nature of the property in question (the demise). It will also detail the remaining period of the lease.

Leaseholders covenants
Covenants are best understood as obligations and responsibilities. Leaseholder's covenants are therefore a list of things that leaseholders should do, such as pay their service charges and keep the interior of the dwelling in good repair and not, for example, to alter the structure. The landlord's covenants will set out the obligations of the

landlord, which is usually to maintain the structure and exterior of the block and light common parts etc.

One unifying theme of all leasehold property is that, notwithstanding the landlord's responsibilities, it is the leaseholder who will pay for everything out of a service charge.

Leases will make detailed provisions for the setting, managing and charging of service charges which should include a section on accounting. All landlords of leaseholders are accountable under the Landlord and Tenant Act 1985, as amended by the 1987 Act and the 2002 Commonhold and Leasehold reform Act. These Acts will regulate the way a landlord treats a leaseholder in the charging and accounting of service charges.

In addition, the 1996 Housing Act and the Commonhold and Leasehold Reform Act 2002 have provided further legislation protecting leaseholders by introducing the right of leaseholders to go to Leasehold Valuation Tribunals if they are unhappy with levels and management of charges and also to carry out audits of charges.

It is vital when buying a leasehold property that you read the lease. Leases tend to be different from each other and nothing can be assumed. When you buy a property, ensure that the person selling has paid all debts and has contributed to some form of "sinking fund" whereby provision has been built up for major repairs in the future. Make sure that you will not be landed with big bills after moving in and that if you are, there is money to deal with them. After a lease has been signed then there is little or no recourse to recoup any money owed.

These are all the finer points of leases and the conveyancer has to be very vigilant. In particular read the schedules to the lease as these sometimes contain rather more detail.

One of the main differences between leasehold and freehold property is that the lease is a long tenancy agreement which contains provisions that give the landlord rather a lot of power to manage (or mismanage) and it is always a possibility that a leaseholder can be forced to give up his or her home in the event of non-compliance with the terms of the lease. This is known as forfeiture.

Under the Commonhold and Leasehold Reform Act 2002 referred to earlier, a new 'no fault right to manage' has been introduced. This will enable leaseholders who are unhappy with the management of their property, to take over the management with relative ease. The Act will apply to most landlords, with the exception of local authorities.

These new powers will go a long way to curb the excesses or inefficiencies of numerous landlords and will provide more control and greater security for leaseholders.

Check points

There are key areas of a lease that should be checked when purchasing. Some have already been discussed.

- What is the term left on the lease?
- Is the preamble clear, i.e. is the area which details landlord, tenant and demised (sold) premises clear?
- Is the lease assignable, i.e. can you pass on the lease without landlords permission or does it need surrendering at sale or a license to assign?
- What is the ground rent and how frequently will you pay it?

- What is the level of service charge, if any, and how is it collected, apportioned, managed and accounted for?
- What are the general restrictions in the lease, can you have pets for example, can you park cars, do you have a designated space?
- What are the respective repairing obligations? As we have seen, the leaseholder will pay anyway but the landlord and leaseholder will hold respective responsibilities. This is an important point because occasionally, there is no stated responsibility for upkeep and the environment deteriorates as a consequence, diminishing the value of the property.

Business leases

Generally, the Landlord and Tenant Act 1954, part 2, provides the framework for those occupying premises on the basis of a business lease. There are a few exceptions to this such as mining leases and agricultural leases. The average business lease will be shorter than a residential lease and will contain periodic rent review clauses. The typical business lease may be for ten years with a rent review after the fifth year.

The whole process of conveyancing business leases, although similar to residential in some respects, is rather more complex. For example, maintenance rights and responsibilities are often an issue between the parties concerned and it is essential that there is a clear picture at the outset. Those coming to the end of the term of their leases can find themselves faced with a significant repair bill, based on a schedule of dilapidations undertaken by a surveyor.

As with all leases, it is very important to ensure that those managing have a firm and comprehensive grasp over the whole process. If they do not then this can affect the value of the property when you wish to sell or buy a lease. It is not advised that an individual undertakes this type of conveyancing, but employs a solicitor well versed in the finer points of business tenancies. 'A Straightforward Guide to Managing Commercial Property', deals with business tenancies in more depth.

Two systems of conveyancing

After gaining an understanding of the nature of the interest in land that you are buying, it is absolutely essential to understand the two systems of conveyancing property in existence, as this will determine, not so much the procedure because the initial basic steps in conveyancing, such as carrying out searches, are common to both forms of land, registered and unregistered, but the way you go about the process and the final registration.

Registered and unregistered land

In England and Wales the method of conveyancing to be used in each particular transaction very much depends on whether the land is registered or unregistered land. If the title, or proof of ownership, of land and property has been registered under the Land Registration Acts 1925-86, as amended, then the Land Registry (see below) will be able to furnish the would-be conveyancer with such documentation as is required to establish ownership, or third party rights etc. If the land has not been registered then proof of ownership of the land in question must be traced through the title deeds.

Registered land

All conveyancing falls within the remit of the Land Registry, because it is compulsory to register land throughout England and Wales. The Land Registration Acts of 1925 established the Land Registry (HM Land Registry). The Land Registry is a department of the Civil Service, at its head is the Chief Land Registrar. Anybody can obtain information which is held on the register of a registered title by going to www.landregistry-search.com. There is a list of fees on this site for the various searches.

There is specific terminology in use within conveyancing, particularly within the Land Registry:

a) A piece of land, or parcel of land is known as a registered title.
b) The owner of land is referred to as the registered proprietor.
c) A conveyance of registered land is called a transfer.
d) A transaction involving registered land is known as a dealing.

The main difference between the two types of conveyancing registered and unregistered concerns what is known as proof of title. In the case of land that is unregistered the owner will prove title by showing the would-be purchaser the documentary evidence which shows how he or she came to own the land and property.

In the case of registered land the owner has to show simply that he or she is registered at the Land Registry as the registered proprietor. Proof of registration is proof of ownership, which is unequivocal. In registered land the documents proving ownership are replaced by the fact of registration. Each separate title or ownership of land has a title number, which the Land Registry uses to trace or confirm ownership. The description of each title on the register is identified by the title number, described by reference to the filed plan (indicating limits and extent of ownership). With registered conveyancing the Land Registry keeps the register of title and file plan. The owner (proprietor) is issued with a Land Certificate. If the land in question is subject to a mortgage then the mortgagor is issued with a Land Certificate.

Production of the Land Certificate

Before the introduction of the Land Registration Act 2002, with registered land, whenever there is a sale, or disposition, then the Land Certificate had to be produced to the Land Registry in the appropriate district. The land Registry no longer produces land or charge certificates.

Now read the key points from chapter 1 overleaf.

KEY POINTS FROM CHAPTER ONE

- Conveyancing is about how to transfer the ownership of land and property from one person to another.

- The process of conveyancing lays down clear procedures for the conveyancer and also sets out each party's position during the process.

- There are two systems of conveyancing-that dealing with registered land and that dealing with unregistered land. Proof of title is easier to establish when land is registered.

- It is compulsory throughout England and Wales to register land-in spite of this a significant amountt of land remains unregistered.

KEY STEPS IN CONVEYANCING – THE INITIAL BASIC SEARCHES

2

THE KEY STEPS IN THE PROCESS OF CONVEYANCING PROPERTY – BASIC SEARCHES

Searches

In chapter's three and four, we will be looking specifically at the processes of conveyancing as they affect registered and unregistered land. However, before we do, it is necessary to look at the processes generally, in order to form a clear idea.

Before the buyer exchanges contracts on a property and then completes the purchase, a number of searches are always carried out. In this chapter we will be looking at four key searches:

1. Enquiries before contract.
2. Local land charges search.
3. Enquiries of the local authority.
4. Index map search.

These are the most essential and common searches and a number of the searches are carried out by the seller. Prior to the abolition of the Home Information packs, local HIPS companies would carry out the searches for you in addition to compiling title deeds etc. However, now that HIPS no longer exist the onus is once again on the seller and the seller's solicitor. Most searches today can be carried out online, for which there is a fee. You should first go to the relevant local authority web page.

Enquiries before contract

These are inquiries to the seller, or the vendor of the property and are aimed at revealing certain facts about the property that the seller has no legal obligation to disclose to the buyer. There are certain matters which are always raised. These are:

- Whether there are any existing boundary disputes.
- What services are supplied to the property, whether electricity, gas or other.
- Any easements or covenants in the lease. These are stipulations in the lease which give other certain rights, such as rights of way.
- Any guarantees in existence.
- Planning considerations.
- Adverse rights affecting the property.
- Any fixtures and fittings.
- Whether there has been any breach of restriction affecting the property.

Please refer to appendix 1 for a sample Purchase statement which lists all the likely charges associated with a purchase of a property when using a solicitor or licensed conveyancer.

The seller's property information forms

If the property is newly built, information will be required concerning any outstanding works or future guarantees of remedying defects. Where a property is leasehold, information will be required about the lessor.

Registered conveyancers will use a standard form to raise these enquiries, so that the initial search is exhaustive. As part of the move towards openness in the process of buying and selling property, and also an attempt to speed up the process of sale, the Law Society introduced forms which the solicitor, or buyer if carrying out his or her own conveyancing, is being encouraged to use. These are Seller's Property Information Form TA6 and TA7 for leasehold information if leasehold. Requisition on title forms are also used. The Law Society Website will give information on what forms are currently used in addition to the aforementioned.

These forms can be obtained from a legal stationers, such as Oyez or, in most cases, from the Land Registry website. See appendix 1 for examples of these forms.

Answers given by the vendor do not form part of the subsequent contract and therefore cannot be used against that person in the event of future problems. However, the Misrepresentations Act of 1976 could be evoked if a deliberate misrepresentation has caused problems.

Local land charges search

The Local Land Charges Act 1975 requires District Councils, London Borough Councils and the City of London Corporation to maintain a Local Land Charges Registry for the area.

A Guide to The Process of Conveyancing

Local land charges can be divided into two areas:
1) Financial charges on the land for work carried out by the local authority
2) Restrictions on the use of land

The register is further divided into twelve parts:

a) General financial charges.
b) Specific financial charges.
c) Planning charges.
d) Miscellaneous charges and provisions.
e) Charges for improvements of ways over fenland.
f) Land compensation charges.
g) New town charges.
h) Civil aviation charges.
i) Open cast coal mining charges.
j) Listed buildings charges.
k) Light obstruction notices.
l) Drainage scheme charges.

All charges are enforceable by the local authority except g and i, which are enforced by statutory bodies and private individuals generally.

A buyer should search in all parts of this particular register and this can be done by a personal or official search. A personal search, as the name suggests, involves the individual or their agent attending at the local authority office, and on paying the relevant fee, personally searching the register. The charges are registered against the land concerned and not against the owner. The official search is the one most favored because, in the event of missing a vital piece of information the chances of compensation are far higher than with a personal search.

With the official search a requisition for a search and for an official certificate of search is sent to the Registrar of Local Land Charges for the area within which the land is situated. There is a fee and the search is carried out by the Registrars staff, which results in a certificate being sent to the person making the request, which clearly outlines any charges.

The Registrar may require a plan of the land as well as the postal address. Separate searches are made of each parcel of land being purchased.

Local authority enquiries

There is a standard form in use for these particular types of searches. This is known as "Con 29R England and Wales" revised August 2007, and the CON290 Optional enquiries of local authorities, with the format of the form differing slightly for inner London boroughs. Any of the forms in the process can be obtained from legal stationers such as Oyez. They can also be purchased from the Law Society.

The standard forms in use contain a statement to the effect that the local authority is not responsible for errors unless negligence is proved. Many of the inquiries relate specifically to planning matters, whilst other elements of the search are concerned about roads and whether they are adopted and whether there are likely to be any costs falling onto property owners. We will be considering planning matters concerning the individual property a little later. Other inquiries relate to possible construction of new roads which may effect the property, the location of sewers and pipes and whether the property is in an area of compulsory registration of title, a smoke controlled area or slum clearance area.

The form used is so constructed that part 2 of the form contains questions, which must be initialed by the purchaser before they are answered. Again these questions cover planning and other matters. Other enquiries can be made by the individual, which are answered at the authorities discretion. In addition to the above, which are the major searches, there are others that the conveyancer has to be aware of. These are as follows:

Searches in the Index map and parcels index of the Land Register

If the land has been registered the title will be disclosed and whether it is registered, leasehold or freehold. Registered rent charges are also disclosed by the search. (See chapter 7)

Commons Registration Act (1965) search

This act imposes a duty on county councils to keep a register relating to village greens and common land and interests over them, such as right of way.

Coal mining search

The request for this search if relevant, is designed to reveal the whereabouts of mineshafts and should be sent to the local area coal board office, or its equivalent. The search will disclose past workings and any subsidence, proposed future workings and the proximity of opencast workings. It is usually well known if there is a problem, or potential problem with coal mining in an area and this search is essential if that is the case.

Other enquiries

There are a number of other bodies from which it might be appropriate to request a search. These include British Rail, Statutory undertakers such as electricity and gas boards, planning authorities generally, rent assessment committees and so on. These will only usually be necessary if there is a direct link between the property being purchased and a particular circumstance within an area or property.

Planning matters relating to specific properties

It is obviously very necessary to determine whether or not any illegal alterations have been carried out to the property you wish to purchase, before reaching the point of exchange of contracts. This is to ensure that the vendor has complied with relevant planning legislation, if any material changes have been made, and that you will not be required at a later date to carry out remedial work. The local authority maintains a register of planning applications relating to properties within their boundaries. In addition, the register will also reveal any planning enforcement notices in force against a particular property.

Questions such as these, and also any questions relating to the effect of structure or local plans, (specific plans relating to local and borough wide plans for the future) should be made in writing to the local authority or an individual search can be carried out. Usually they are carried out if there is any suspicion that planning regulations may have been breached. In addition, there may be other considerations, such as whether the building is listed or whether tree preservation orders relating to trees within the cartilage of the property are in force. It is certainly essential to know about these.

It is highly recommended that all of these searches are carried out and completed before contracts are exchanged.

Now read the key points from chapter two.

****

KEY POINTS FROM CHAPTER TWO

- Before the buyer exchanges contracts on a property it is essential to carry out a number of key searches.

- In addition to the main searches, there are a number of ancillary searches which should be made if appropriate.

- There are standard forms for carrying out such searches-if you are doing your own conveyancing these can be obtained from any legal stationers, such as Oyez.

- There may be other considerations such as conservation or planning issues that need to be looked into.

3

THE STRUCTURAL SURVEY

Anyone who purchases a property should carry out a structural survey. This is highly advisable and preferably will be as in-depth as possible. A chartered surveyor should be used. If a qualified surveyor is negligent when compiling his or her report of the property then that person can be sued. Most residential property is purchased with assistance from a building society or bank. The lender will insist on a survey before lending the money in order to protect their advance. However, this survey is cursory at the best and will not reveal more serious problems. Therefore, at this point in the conveyancing process, the person purchasing, or the person acting on his or her behalf should ensure that they are thoroughly acquainted with the condition of the property. If you are purchasing a house which is in the course of construction, then there will be the benefit of a warranty of good work and proper materials so that the house will be fit for habitation. This protection does not extend to any subsequent purchasers. There is however, a form of statutory protection under the Defective Premises Act of 1972 which imposes a duty on a developer and those associated with the developer to build in a correct manner. The Act covers anyone acquiring an interest in a dwelling.

The National House Builders Scheme

This scheme was redrafted in 1979 and in 1988 the Buildmark scheme was introduced. Builders who are registered with the NHBS must offer a warranty to first and subsequent purchasers, that, essentially, has a ten-year shelf life from date of construction. During the first two years from issue the builder is liable to make good any defects due to non-compliance with NHBS regulations. The first two years are known as the initial guarantee period. After this, the remaining eight years are referred to as the structural guarantee period. During this time the NHBS will reimburse the purchaser the cost of remedying major works caused by any defect in the structure or subsidence, settlement or heave, provided that there is no other insurance at the time of the claim to cover the cost.

Liability of the builder outside the two year period

The NHBS agreement states that if any work undertaken by the builder in the initial guarantee period to remedy a defect caused by the breach of the NHBS requirements fails to remedy the defect or damage, the vendor/builder will remain under a continuing liability to remedy the damage after the initial guarantee period.

Conveyancing a property is not just about successfully reaching a conclusion in a sale. It is also about ensuring that the property you are buying is sound and that you make sure that you have a clear picture of what you are buying, preferably by obtaining a report from a chartered surveyor. Now read the key points from chapter three.

KEY POINTS FROM CHAPTER THREE

- Anyone who purchases a property must carry out a structural survey. It is essential that a qualified surveyor is used.

- If you are purchasing a house under construction there will be the benefit of a warranty with the property.

- The National House Builders Scheme offers a warranty for ten years for those who purchase a house/flat from a registered developer.

PROOF OF TITLE AND OTHER SEARCHES – UNREGISTERED LAND

4

CONVEYANCING UNREGISTERED LAND

We have considered the processes of conveyancing generally and the searches common to all property. However, it is now necessary to look at the specifics of conveyancing registered and unregistered land.

With unregistered land, as we have seen, there is a duty on the vendor to prove his or her title to the land, i.e., that they own the land in question. If all is registered at the Land Registry then life can be a good deal simpler. However, if not, then the process can be more complex.

The abstract of title - unregistered land. Establishing proof of ownership

The abstract of title is an epitome of the various documents and events which together demonstrate that the vendor has good title to the land, conclusively owns the land. The vendor must, at his or her own expense, produce and deliver a proper abstract of title to the purchaser, unless there is an agreement to do otherwise, which would be unusual.

The abstract starts with the root or the origin of title. Every deed which dealt with transactions relating to this property subsequently must be abstracted. A conveyance relating to the purchase of the freehold is the strongest form of root of title, likewise a mortgage deed relating to that conveyance. If a vendor has lost any of the titles which relate to the land then it is usual for the vendor to insert a special condition into the contract stating what secondary evidence will be produced to prove title. Secondary evidence can be in the form of a counterpart lease, for example.

Once the abstract has been delivered, the purchaser must examine these documents against the originals. The purpose of the examination is to ensure that what has been abstracted has been properly or correctly abstracted, ensure that each document has been properly executed, attested and stamped and that there have been no changes to the title, such as memoranda endorsed on deeds or documents. Any doubt as to the validity of the title should be raised with the vendor's solicitor directly and promptly by written requisition. The purchaser is entitled to raise requisitions on any part of the title which is unsatisfactory, for example, if the title discloses a mortgage or covenant which was not disclosed in the contract. An omission from the abstract may be remedied by an answer to the requisition. The expense of verification of this answer is the purchaser's. The purchaser can serve a notice on the vendor requiring him to furnish an answer by a given date. Failure to reply by this date entitles the purchaser to rescind the contract. If the purchaser is still not satisfied with the vendor's replies, he or she can send observations back to the vendor relating to the reply.

There is a standard condition of sale, which states that the vendor can rescind the sale if he or she cannot furnish a reasonable reply to the requisition. This right however, is based on reasonable grounds, i.e., inability or unwillingness to answer.

Pre-completion searches

We discussed the key searches to be carried out prior to exchange and completion in the previous chapter. There are, however, other searches necessary, depending on the status of the property. With unregistered property, some of these searches involve the Land Registry.

The purchaser or agent should carry out various searches immediately before completion in order to determine whether there are any encumbrances affecting the vendor's title to the property. The most important of these is the Land Charges Register of the Land Charges Department of the Land Registry.

There are five registers in total:
a) The register of pending actions. This registers any actions that may be pending against that title.
b) The register of annuities. This registers any rent charge or other charge such as an annuity against the land.
c) The registry of writs and orders. This register is concerned with the registering and enforcing of any orders against land.
d) The register of deeds and arrangements. This is concerned with trustees or creditors who may benefit from that particular title.
e) The register of land charges.

The Register of Land charges
This is the most important register and the charges are classified as follows:
a) Class A (s2(2). These are charges upon land, created by statute, which only come into existence after the appropriate person has made an application under the particular statute. Once created they may be registered against the estate owner.
b) Class B (s2(3). These are similar charges to those in class A.
c) Class C is subdivided as follows:

d) A puisne mortgage, i.e., a legal mortgage not being protected by
the deposit of documents relating to the legal estate affected.
a limited owner's charge, an equitable charge acquired by a
tenant for life by a statutory owner by statute because he
has paid taxes or other liability related to the estate.

ii) A general equitable charge. This is a sweeping up charge,
including all charges not protected by the deposit of title deeds etc.

iii) An estate contract. This is an estate contract by someone
who is entitled at the date of contract to have the legal
estate conveyed to him, to convey or create a legal estate.

d) Class D, this is a charge on land acquired by the
commissioners of the Inland Revenue for unpaid capital
transfer taxes.

e) Class E .This class covers annuities.

f) Class F covers charges affecting the matrimonial home by
virtue of a spouses rights of occupation under the
Matrimonial Homes Act 1983 as amended by the Family
Law Act 1996.

Methods of making a land charges search

A search may be made in person, by post, or by telephone. Personal
searches should not be made as this should be left to those who know
the system and are employed to carry out searches.

A postal search effective for all registers is made on a form PIC.
The information required for a postal search is the name of the estate
owner, period of years searched against, address, county and
description of property. Completed searches are usually sent back
promptly. If the search reveals an adverse entry then the purchaser
should ensure that the property concerned is not affected.

Other searches

Company searches are usually necessary if the property to be purchased is from a company. Company agents can ascertain whether there is a winding up order against the company or whether there are any specific charges relating to that company registered against the title to land.

The nature of the conveyance

It should be noted that if land to be conveyed is in an area of compulsory registration at the Land Registry, as most land is, the purchasers solicitor may, instead of preparing the traditional form of conveyance as described below, utilise the much simpler form of a registered land transfer. For more details concerning this form see chapter five. For those whose property will not be immediately registered the following applies.

The purchaser's solicitor will prepare a draft conveyance in duplicate and send it to the vendor's solicitor for scrutiny and approval. The vendor's solicitor will normally send back a copy with amendments in red pen. When the deed is agreed (settled) the purchaser's solicitor has it engrossed (fair copied) and then sends it to the vendor's solicitor to keep until the day of completion.

The contents of a typical conveyance of unregistered land

An example conveyance is shown further on in this chapter. The heading of the document will begin with the words "This conveyance" or "This deed of gift" etc. The conveyance is dated and the full names of the parties are inserted along with their addresses. If there are parties other than the vendor and purchaser, for example, any trustees, they are also inserted.

The Recital

This part of the deed will usually begin "whereas" and the purpose is to outline a history of transactions related to that property. They are largely unnecessary and are there as a result of tradition as it has evolved in conveyancing.

The Testatum

The testatum is part of the operative part of the conveyance and will begin with "Now this deed witnesses".

The formal words are followed by a statement of consideration for the transaction and a receipt by the vendor for the purchase money. No other receipt is required, although this does not stop a vendor challenging the fact that a receipt has been paid.

Words of grant

These are the words which pass the vendor's estate to the purchaser. The usual form of words will state "The vendor as beneficial owner hereby conveys". There will then be a description of the property conveyed, known as the parcels clause.

In a lease there will be what is known as a reddendum, which goes on to describe rent and rent days.

There are also what is known as covenants, either negative or positive covenants, which impose obligations, or rights on either party. In modern developments these conveyances are usually very lengthy and are contained in a schedule to the deed.

Where a vendor remains liable on a covenant after sale he or she should ensure that the purchaser enters into a covenant to indemnify the vendor in respect of any liability arising from a future breach of that covenant. The effect is to indemnify the vendor against any loss or expenses in respect of breach of covenant. Where the property is conveyed to joint tenants a clause is very often included declaring that each tenant holds joint equity and conferring on the co-owners additional powers of dealing with the land in question.

The testimonium

This is the formal clause, which precedes the party's execution of the deed and will typically be worded " In witness where of the parties here to have executed this document as their deed the day and year first before mentioned".

Execution of deeds before July 31st 1990

The Law of Property Act 1989 introduced very important changes in the execution of deeds. Under the Law of Property Act 1925 three formal requirements for a deed are outlined, namely that it must be signed sealed and delivered. The effective date of the deed is the effective date of delivery. However, after 1989 a seal is no longer required, just an effective signature, signed before a witness. The Companies Act 1989 also allows for companies to execute a deed by signature, with a seal no longer a requirement.

Completion of sale of unregistered land

The date for completion will be stated in the contract. See chapter 6. Usually, completion will take place at the offices of the vendor's solicitor. If there is an outstanding mortgage on the property and the mortgagee will not release the deeds to the vendors solicitor until after it is discharged then completion will take place at the mortgagees solicitor. Completion allows for settling of the financial account between vendor and purchaser and completion of legal work plus handing over the executed deed. Money is usually sent from a bank to the solicitor. Deeds are usually examined a last time to see that all is correct. The vendor may retain part of a title deed if there is any ongoing involvement, i.e., part ownership of land etc.

In unregistered conveyancing the legal estate is vested in the purchaser. The purchaser is also entitled to possession of the property and the solicitors should ensure that adequate arrangements have been made to this end.

Where the vendor is selling as a personal representative of another, a memoranda of sale should be endorsed on the grant of representation which he or she will have. Where the purchaser enters into covenants for the protection of land retained or is granted additional rights, such as rights over land, it is common for the vendor to retain a duplicate copy (counterpart).

Example of conveyance of unregistered land

This CONVEYANCE BY DEED is made the day of 2013 between J Smith of 19 Jupiter Street, Othertown (hereinafter called the vendor) of one part and F Deal of 1 Mars Street Eithertown (hereinafter called the purchaser) of the other part.
WHEREAS

(1) The vendor is seised of the property hereinafter described for an estate in fee simple in possession free from encumbrances and as hereinafter mentioned and has agreed with the purchaser for the sale to him of the said property for a like estate for a price of seventy five thousand pounds

NOW THIS DEED WITNESSETH

1._____ In pursuance of the said agreement and in consideration of the sum of <u>seventy five thousand pounds</u> now paid by the purchaser to the vendor (the receipt of which sum the vendor hereby acknowledges) the vendor as beneficial owner hereby conveys unto the purchaser all that land and property known as 41 Otherplace, Othertown as was conveyed to the vendor by John Rarer by a conveyance of 25th May 1952 and is further therein more particularly described and subject to the covenants therein contained but otherwise free from encumbrances <u>TO HOLD</u> the same unto the purchaser in fee simple_____

2. <u>With</u> the object and intent of affording to the vendor a full and sufficient indemnity but not further or otherwise the purchaser hereby covenants with the vendor to observe and perform the above mentioned covenant and to indemnify the vendor against all actions claims demands and liabilities in respect thereof _____

3. <u>It is hereby</u> certified that the transaction affected does not form part of a larger transaction or of a series of transactions in respect of which the amount or value or the aggregate amount or value of the consideration exceeds eighty pounds_____

   <u>IN WITNESS</u> whereof the parties hereto have executed this document as their deed the day and year first before written.

<u>EXECUTED AS HIS DEED</u>
By the aforementioned

J Smith in the presence of   ) J Smith
K Knowles   )
46 hilltop   )
Otherplace

EXECUTED AS HIS DEED

By the aforementioned
John Rarer in the presence of   ) John Rarer
K Smile   )
42 Child Street
Cidertown   )

Now read the key points from chapter four.

KEY POINTS FROM CHAPTER FOUR

- The purchasers solicitor will prepare a draft in conveyance in duplicate and send in duplicate to the vendors solicitor for scrutiny and approval.

- When the deal is agreed, the purchaser's solicitor has it engrossed and then sends it to the vendor's solicitor until completion.

- Deeds executed after July 31st 1990 do not require a seal.

- The date for completion should be clearly stated in the contract.

- Completion allows for the settling of the financial account between vendor and purchaser.

5

CONVEYANCING REGISTERED LAND – PROCESSES PRIOR TO COMPLETION

In chapter four, we looked at the general process of conveyancing unregistered land. In this chapter we will concentrate on registered land. In all likelihood, you will be dealing with registered land as most property is now registered.

First Registration of title

First registration of land may take place voluntarily or compulsorily depending on the nature of the transaction. Land Registry form FR1 should be used. Compulsory registration now extends to most of England and Wales. It is highly undesirable to complete a sale of land and then neglect to register it.

When a sale is completed an application must be lodged for registration within two months of completion. The effect of non-registration is that the deed of transfer, or the conveyance, becomes null and void after the two-month period. In other words, there is no choice but to register the land.

Under s123 of the Law of Property Act, the Chief Land Registrar may accept a late registration. An explanation of why the property was not registered within the time period will be required. Acceptance of the application has the effect of registering the estate to the purchaser from the date of completion. Late applications are rarely refused.

When land is purchased in a compulsory area but the title is not yet registered, even where the transaction must be followed by a first registration the procedure until completion is identical to the procedure in unregistered conveyancing. The purchaser will know that he must effect a first registration from the form 96 search of the index map, as outlined. In addition the reply to one of the standard enquiries of the district council within which the land is situated will reveal whether or not the land is in an area of compulsory registration. In effect, as stated, most land is in an area of compulsory registration.

The purchaser's solicitor will forward the correct form to the land registry. For a first registration of freehold land form 1A is used.

This form is called a "cover" because it is double sided and when folded will contain all the necessary documentation for registration. The cover will contain a certificate signed by a solicitor that the title has been properly investigated, a statement that any land charges entries revealed by the official search either do or do not affect the land concerned and if they do a note of the document by which they were created. In addition, a schedule of encumbrances affecting the property is sent.

All the original deeds and other documents of title must be sent. Enough information by way of plan must be sent to enable registry staff to fix the position of the property on the Ordnance Survey Map. There is a prescribed fee which the Land Registry can provide details of on request.

For application by the owner for first registration of leasehold land other than on the grant of a new lease and for application by the owner for first registration of leasehold land on grant of a new lease, see appendix for forms.

Outline of the Land Registry and the registration process

In registered land the documents of title are replaced by the fact of registration. Therefore, the equivalent to the title deed is the various entries in the Land Registry.

Each title is given a title number, which is then used to trace title. The description of each title is identified by a title number, described by reference to a filed plan and a set of index cards retained to record specifics about that title.

The index cards and the filed plan are the equivalent of title deeds. The registered proprietor is issued with a land certificate containing a facsimile copy of the registered title. If land within a particular title number is subject to a mortgage the land certificate is retained by the Registry and the mortgagee is instead issued with a charge certificate, and the land certificate is retained by the Land Registry.

There are three registers of title at the Land Registry, the Property Register, The Proprietorship Register and the Charges Register.

The Property Register is similar to the Parcels Clause in unregistered conveyancing i.e. it describes the land in question. It will identify the geographical location and extent of the registered property by means of a short description and a reference to an official plan, which is prepared for each title. It may also give particulars of any rights that benefit the land, for example, a right of way over adjoining land. In the case of a lease the register will also describe the parties to the lease, the term and the rent, any exceptions or reservations from the lease and, if the lessors title is registered, the title number.

The Proprietorship Register is similar to the Habendum in unregistered conveyancing. It will describe the type of title, i.e., title absolute, leasehold etc, the full name and address of the registered proprietor, description of that person, date of registration, price paid for the property and any other relevant entries. There will also be any relevant cautions, inhibitions or restrictions entered on the Register.

The Charges Register contains any encumbrances affecting the registered property, such as mortgages and any other charges taken over the property. However, details of the amount of money involved are not disclosed.

How to inspect the Register

The Land Registry has an online conveyancing system. Normally, solicitors use this and evidence of title can be deduced by going into the web site. Evidence of title can also be obtained by writing to the Land Registry.

If you wish, after you have received the copies of the register that you require, you can, by filling in the appropriate forms (see appendix 1) obtain copies of documents that you would like to inspect. Again, a fee is payable. If you only wish to know the name and address of the registered proprietor of a property, you should fill in Land Registry form PN1. You should then phone the Land Registry Customer Support Team on 0844 892 1111. They will direct you to the relevant office to send the form to.

The Land/Charge Certificate

Prior to 2003, when a title was registered for the first time or changed hands, a Land Certificate was issued by the Land Registry. The Land Certificate was regarded as the equivalent to the title deed although this can be misleading as it is only a facsimile of the official register and may not be up to date. In addition, there may be matters of title not contained on the register. The Land Certificate had to be produced to the appropriate Land Registry whenever there is a sale or transfer of land. A Charge Certificate had to be produced too.

As mentioned in the introduction, following the introduction of the Land Registration Act 2002, and the practice of 'dematerialisation' Land and Charge Certificates have now been abolished. If you have lost your certificate you do not need to replace it. Electronic copies of the land certificate can now be obtained through the Land Registry website.

Maps and descriptions of land

The Index map and parcels index provides that a map should be kept showing the position and extent of all registered titles. This is called the Public Index Map. This is open to inspection by any person, and can be inspected personally or by official search (see appendix). There will be a fee for this search.

All registered land must, in addition, be described by the applicant in such a way as to enable the land to be fully identified on the ordnance map or general map.

The Land Registry uses a consistent colour coding on its plans. This does not vary and it is expected that solicitors when preparing plans will use the same system. The colouring scheme is as follows:

- Red edging marks the extent of land within a particular title.
- Green tinting shows excluded pieces of land within the area of the title.
- Brown tinting shows land over which the registered land has a right of way.
- Blue tinting shows land within the title subject to a right of way.

For further references, colours are used in the following order:

a) Tinting in pink, blue yellow and mauve.
b) Edging with a blue yellow or mauve band.
c) Hatching with a colour other than black or green.
d) Numbering or lettering of small self contained areas.

In addition, when reading a filed plan it should be noted that a boundary represented by a feature shown on the ground or on the existing ordnance survey is represented by a continuous dark line. A boundary not representing such a feature is shown by a broken dark line.

The scale of the filed plan is usually 1/1250 enlarged from the survey 1/2500.

Now read the key points from chapter five.

KEY POINTS FROM CHAPTER FIVE

- Registered conveyancing entails the owner simply demonstrating that the registered proprietorship is recorded at the Land Registry.

- Each title is given a title number, which is described by reference to a filed plan and a set of Index Cards. These are the equivalent of title deeds

- There are three registers of title at the Land Registry, The Property Register, The Proprietorship Register and The Charges Register.

- The best and most convenient way of obtaining details from the Register is by post on Land Registry form number 109.

- First registration of land may take place voluntarily or be compulsory depending on the nature of the transaction.

THE CONTRACT FOR SALE –
EXCHANGE AND COMPLETION

6

THE CONTRACT FOR SALE

Forming the contract

Having discussed the processes involved in conveying registered and unregistered land, prior to exchange and completion, it is now necessary to look at the contract for sale, which is formulated at the outset but not exchanged or completed before all parties are satisfied with the prior processes of conveyancing.

As with many other transactions, a sale of land is effected through a contract. However, a contract, which deals with the sale of land, is governed by the requirements of the Law of Property (miscellaneous provisions) Act 1989, the equitable doctrine of specific performance and the duty of the vendor to provide title to the property.

The Law of Property Act (miscellaneous provisions) 1989 provides that contracts dealing with the sale of land after 26th September 1989 must be in writing. The contract must contain all the terms and agreements to which the respective parties to the transaction have agreed. The provisions of the Act do not apply to sales at a public auction, contracts to grant a short lease and contracts regulated under the Financial Services Act 1986. If the person purchasing is doing so through an agent then the agent must have authority to act on behalf of the purchaser. Examples of agents are auctioneers, solicitors and estate agents.

Agreements

If the phrase "subject to contract" is used in a sale then the intention of both parties to the contract is that neither are contractually bound until a formal contract has been agreed by the parties, signed and exchanged. Therefore, the words "subject to contract" are a protective device, although it is not good to depend on the use of these words throughout a transaction.

Procedures in the formation of contract

The vendor's solicitor will usually draw up an initial contract of sale. This is because only this person has access to all the necessary initial documents to begin to effect a contract. The draft contract is prepared in two parts and sent to the purchaser's solicitor (if using a solicitor) the other side will approve or amend the contract as necessary. Both sides must agree to any proposed amendments. (see standard letters used in process of conveyancing appendix 1). After agreement has been reached, the vendor's solicitor will retain one copy of the contract and send the other copy to the solicitor or person acting for the other side. The next stage is for the vendor's solicitor to engross (sign and formalise) the contract in two parts. Both parts are then sent to the purchaser's solicitor or other agent who checks that they are correct then sends one part back to the vendor's solicitor.

Signing the contract

The vendor's solicitor will obtain the vendor's signature to the contract, when he is satisfied that the vendor can sell what he is purporting to do through the contract. The purchaser's solicitor or agent will do the same, having checked the replies to all inquiries before contract. It is also essential to check that a mortgage offer has been made and accepted.

Signing the Transfer

The transfer (form TR1-see appendix) is the document transferring ownership of the property to the buyer. It confirms the details set out in the contract. The transfer is sent out by the solicitor (see standard letters appendix 1) for you to sign in readiness for exchange and completion.

Exchanging contracts

Neither party to the sale is legally bound until there has been an exchange of contracts. At one time, a face-to-face exchange would have taken place. However, with the rapid increases in property transactions this rarely happens nowadays. Exchange by post or telephone is more common. The purchaser will post his or her part of the contract together with the appropriate cheque, or bank transfer, to cover the agreed deposit to the purchaser's solicitor or person acting on behalf of that person. The deposit is usually 10% of the purchase price although there are variations on this theme. The amounts are agreed between buyer and seller. The purchaser's solicitor will usually insert the agreed completion date. On receiving this part of the contract the vendor will add his or her part and send this off in exchange. At this stage, both parties become bound under the contract.

The Contents of a contract

A contract will be in two parts, the particulars of sale and the conditions of sale. The particulars of sale give a physical description of the land and also of the interest which is being sold. A property must be described accurately and a plan may be attached to the contract to emphasise or illustrate what is in the contract. The particulars will also outline whether the property is freehold or leasehold and what kind of lease the vendor is assigning, i.e., head lease (where vendor is owner of the freehold) or underlease, (where the vendor is not).

It is very important to determine what kind of lease it is that is being assigned, indeed whether it is assignable or whether permission is needed from the landlord and it is recommended that a solicitor handle this transaction. This is because any purchaser of a lease can find his or her interest jeopardised by the nature of the lease. Where a sub-lease, or under lease is being purchased, the purchasers interest can be forfeited by the actions of the head lessee, the actions of this person being out of control of the purchaser.

Rights, such as easements and also restrictive covenants, which are for the benefit of the land, should be expressly referred to in the particulars of sale. In addition, the vendor should refer to any latent defects affecting his or her property, if known. This includes any encumbrances, which may affect the property.

Misdescription

If the property in the particulars of sale is described wrongly, i.e. there is a misstatement of fact, such as describing leasehold as freehold land, calling an under-lease a lease or leaving out something that misleads the buyer, in other words, if the mis description is material, then the purchaser is entitled to rescind the contract. Essentially the contract must describe what is being sold and if it does not, and the buyer is mislead then the contract is inaccurate.

If the misdescription is immaterial and insubstantial, and there has been no misrepresentation then the purchaser cannot rescind the contract. However, if the misdescription has affected the purchase price of the property then the purchaser can insist on a reduction in the asking price. The purchaser should claim this compensation before completion takes place.

The vendor has no right to rescind the contract if the misdescription is in the purchaser's favor, for example, the area of land sold is greater than that intended. Neither can the vendor compel the purchaser to pay an increased purchase price.

Misrepresentation

Misrepresentation is an untrue statement of fact made by one party or his or her agent, which induces the other party to enter into the contract. An opinion and a statement of intention must be distinguished from a statement of fact. There are three types of misrepresentation, fraudulent misrepresentation, negligent misrepresentation and innocent misrepresentation. Fraudulent misrepresentation is a false statement made knowingly or without belief in its truth, or recklessly. The innocent party may sue through the tort of negligence either before or after the contract is complete and rescind the contract. Negligent misrepresentation, although not fraudulent, is where the vendor or his or her agents cannot prove that the statement they made in relation to the contract was correct. Remedies available are damages or rescission of the contract. Innocent misrepresentation is where the statement made was neither fraudulently or negligently but is still an untrue statement. Rescission is available for this particular type of misrepresentation.

Rescission of contract generally is available under the Misrepresentation Act 1967 s 2(2).

Non-disclosure

Generally, in the law of contract, there is the principle of "caveat emptor" "let the buyer beware". In other words, it is up to the purchaser to ensure that what he or she is buying is worth the money paid for it. Earlier we talked about the importance of searches and also, particularly, the importance of the structural survey. Although the vendor has some responsibility to reveal any defects in the property it is always very advisable for the purchaser to ensure that all checks prior to purchase are carried out thoroughly.

Conditions of sale

There are two types of conditions, special conditions and general conditions. Special conditions are those which are specific to an individual contract, such as when a specific day is fixed for completion. The general conditions are those which have general application.

General conditions of sale are standard entitled, "National protocol for domestic leasehold and freehold property." This is a complete guide to conveyancing in itself and can be obtained from the Law Society. The Law Society has recently updated this protocol.

The general conditions of sale oblige the vendor to supply the purchaser with abstracts or any copies of a lease or agreement in writing. The vendor must always supply the purchaser with details of any tenancy agreements in existence. A deposit for the purchase will only be payable if there is a special or general condition to this effect, such a term is not implied into a contract. Under standard conditions a deposit of 10 percent of the purchase price is paid to the vendor's solicitor prior to purchase but this can be varied between parties. The deposit should be in cash or by banker's draft at the date of the contract (exchange). Failure to pay, or payment by a cheque, which is subsequently dishonored, is a breach and can lead to the vendor rescinding the contract. The general conditions specifically refer to this.

If there is any interest due, or expected on purchase money this will be dealt with in the special conditions of contract.

Completion

The requirements concerning completion are detailed thoroughly in the general conditions of sale. Payment on completion is one such detail. Payment on completion should be by one of the following methods:

- Legal tender.
- Bankers draft.
- An unconditional authority to release any deposit by the stakeholder.
- Any other method agreed with the vendor.

At common law, completion takes place whenever the vendor wishes and payment is to be made by legal tender.

Also dealt with in the general conditions is failure to complete and notices to complete. Failure to complete can cause difficulty for one of the other parties and the aggrieved party can serve notice on the other to complete by a specific date.

The notice has the effect of making "time of the essence" which means that a specific date is attached to completion, after which the contract is discharged.

Return of deposits

The vendor must return any deposit paid to the purchaser if the purchaser drops out before the exchange of contracts. This cannot be prevented and was the subject of a House of Lords ruling in the 1977 case Sorrel v Finch.

The position of the parties after exchange of contracts

Once a contract has been exchanged the purchaser is the beneficial owner of the property, with the vendor owning the property on trust for the purchaser. The vendor is entitled to any rents or other profits from the land during this period, and has the right to retain the property until final payments have been made and has a lien (charge/right) over the property in respect of any unpaid purchase monies.

The vendor is bound to take reasonable care of the property and should not let the property fall into disrepair or other damages to be caused during the period between exchange and completion. If completion does not take place at the allotted time and the fault is the purchasers then interest can be charged on the money due.

The purchaser, as beneficial owner of the property is entitled to any increase in the value of the land and buildings but not profits arising. The purchaser has a right of lien over the property, the same as the vendor, in respect of any part of the purchase price paid prior to completion.

Bankruptcy of the vendor

In the unfortunate event of the vendor going bankrupt in between exchange and completion, the normal principles of bankruptcy apply so that the trustee in bankruptcy steps in to the vendor's shoes. The purchaser can be compelled to complete the sale. The trustee in bankruptcy is obliged to complete the sale if the purchaser tenders the purchase money on the completion day.

Bankruptcy of the purchaser

When a purchaser is declared bankrupt in between sale and completion, all of his or her property vests in the trustee in bankruptcy. The trustee can compel the vendor to complete the transaction by paying monies due by the allotted day. If the vendor wishes to proceed with the sale and the trustee is reluctant, the trustee has the right to claim that the contract is onerous. However, in these circumstances, the vendor can keep any deposit due to him. A form for bankruptcy purchases is shown in appendix 1.

Death of the vendor or the purchaser

The personal representatives of a deceased vendor can compel the purchaser to sell. The money is conveyed to those representatives who will hold the money in accordance with the terms of any will or in accordance with the rules relating to intestacy if there is no will.

The same position applies to the purchaser's representatives, who can be compelled by the vendor to complete the purchase and who can hold money on the purchaser's behalf.

Other factors in the conveyancing process

Obtaining proof of identity

Solicitors are obliged by law to obtain evidence of those who intend to sell or purchase property. This is in line with regulations published in the Council of Mortgage Lenders Handbook-dealing with money laundering. The documents supplied (listed below) have to be certified either by a solicitor or the estate agent dealing with the sale. The post office can also verify the documents for a small fee.

You will need to prove identification and address.

Proof of identity

This can be your passport or photo card driving licence. A copy may be acceptable if it is certified as a true likeness by a regulated person.

Proof of address

This can be a utility bill less than three months old, a council tax demand or bank statement.

The solicitor in question will supply you with a list of acceptable documents.

Cash is not acceptable

Because of money laundering regulations, solicitors can only accept payments into bank accounts if they are from a UK bank or building society. If they are received from any other source then the solicitor is under an obligation to report the matter to the Serious Organized Crime Agency (SOCA).

Repaying a mortgage

If there is a mortgage on the property in question, this must be redeemed (paid off) on completion of the sale. Even if the mortgage is 'portable' then it still has to be paid off. A redemption statement has to be obtained from the lender, detailing the amount outstanding from that lender against that property. You should take into account any redemption penalties. The redemption statement is usually obtained at the beginning of the conveyance and then again at exchange of contracts.

Negative equity

If the amount to repay your mortgage is higher than the sale price contracts cannot be exchanged until any shortfall has been made up.

In virtually all cases, the mortgage is repaid in full on the day of completion by electronic transfer.

Now read the key points from chapter six.

KEY POINTS FROM CHAPTER SIX

- As with many other transactions, a sale of land is affected through a contract. The Law of Property Act, (Miscellaneous Provisions) 1988 provides that contracts dealing with the sale of land after 26th September 1989, must be in writing.

- If the phrase "subject to contract" is used then the intention of both parties to the contract is that neither are contractually bound until a formal contract has been agreed, signed and exchanged by the parties.

- Neither party is legally bound until there has been an exchange of contracts.

- Contracts are in two parts, The Particulars of Sale and the Conditions of Sale. The particulars give a physical description of the land and interest. There are two types of conditions, special and general. The latter is governed by the National Protocol for Domestic Leasehold and Freehold Property.

7

POST COMPLETION REGISTERED AND UNREGISTERED LAND

Completion of a land transaction will usually happen in the office of the vendor's solicitor. If there is an outstanding mortgage on the property and the mortgagee will not release the deeds until after payment has been made then completion will take place in the mortgagee's solicitors premises.

Completion will entail settling any outstanding payments between the vendor and purchaser. Also any legal work will be completed and deeds, if appropriate will be handed over.

On every transfer of sale of a freehold, lease or under-lease of seven years or more, the purchaser must complete a form giving particulars to the Inland Revenue. The form is to register the property for stamp duty and is known as "Stamps l (A) 451" or the "Particulars Delivered" form.

If the land is registered or being registered for the first time after completion, then if there is no stamp duty land tax (SDLT) payable the particulars must be sent to the Land Registry together with an application for registration. In every other case, the deed and the particulars delivered form must be sent to the Inland Revenue within thirty days of completion.

Stamp duty current rates:

Residential land or property SDLT rates and thresholds

Purchase price/lease premium or transfer value	SDLT rate
Up to £125,000	Zero
Over £125,000 to £250,000	1%
Over £250,000 to £500,000	3%
Over £500,000 to £1 million	4%
Over £1 million to £2 million	5%
Over £2 million from 22 March 2012	7%
Over £2 million (purchased by certain persons including corporate bodies) from 21 March 2012	15%

Properties bought in a disadvantaged area

Disadvantaged Areas Relief will be abolished for transactions with an effective date on or after 6 April 2013.

All claims to this relief must be made on or before 5 May 2014. Claims made after that date will not be accepted.

If the property is in an area designated by the government as 'disadvantaged' a higher threshold of £150,000 applies for residential properties.

Disadvantaged areas - residential land or property SDLT rates and thresholds

Purchase price/lease premium or transfer value	SDLT rate
Up to £150,000	Zero
Over £150,000 to £250,000	1%
Over £250,000 to £500,000	3%
Over £500,000 to £1 million	4%
Over £1 million to £2 million	5%
Over £2 million from 22 March 2012	7%
Over £2 million (purchased by certain persons including corporate bodies) from 21 March 2012	15%

An application must be made to the Land Registry to register the transaction. This will involve sending:

1. The fee
2. The transfer form TR1 which is used in all cases where the transfer of a title has happened.
3. Evidence of any previous mortgage being paid off.
4. Details of the new charge by the delivery of a copy of the mortgage and original mortgage.

The title can then be registered in the name of the new purchaser together with details of any new charge.

Once registration is complete a copy should be sent to the purchaser for checking and any original documents should be sent to the lender for safekeeping.

CONCLUSION

This book is intended to be a guide to the processes of conveyancing and should be used in conjunction with a solicitor.

The book is very much about the procedures involved in buying and selling property. However, unless a conveyance is likely to be straightforward then you are advised to employ a solicitor or licensed conveyancer to carry out the work. Prices for such work are quite often very competitive and if there is a problem along the way then at least you have redress after the event.

Summary of process
We saw in chapter two that there are basic searches common to all properties that must be carried out prior to exchange of contracts. In chapter three we discussed the importance of carrying out a structural survey before committing to a purchase. In chapter four we discussed the various issues concerning unregistered land and the need to prove title and to carry out further additional searches. In chapter five we discussed the issues surrounding registered land and proof of title. Finally we discussed the contract for sale and process of completion following the various stages of conveyancing of land. Standard letters relating to each of these stages are contained within appendix 1. The standard forms used are contained within appendix 2.

A few simple words of advice:
When buying property make sure that all debts are paid by the vendor before completing. This is especially pertinent to leasehold property that is quite often subject to a service charge. If the vendor

does not settle debts then the purchaser will find his or herself taking on the debt. Read contracts/leases very carefully indeed. Make sure that you know what it is that you are buying and that you are fully aware. Buying and selling property is a complex task-be very cautious and always scrutinise all documents very carefully. Make sure that what you buy is in sound condition and represents a good investment. It is the biggest investment that you will probably make.

Glossary

A

Acting for both parties

There are limited circumstances when solicitors can act for both parties

Amount outstanding on the mortgage

Also known as the redemption figure

Apportionment of the purchase price

This may be used to save stamp duty land tax Fixtures and fittings known as chattels do not attract stamp duty and this is why the distinction between those and land is important.

Attorneys

A deed may be signed by an attorney but evidence of his power of attorney must be produced as this will be required by the land registry.

Auctions

The auction contract is usually prepared in advance The purchaser has the right to undertake all his searches en enquiries and survey before the auction. Once the auction has been concluded usually a ten per cent deposit is taken and the sale takes place 28 days later. It would be necessary for anyone entering into an auction to have their finance in place before the hammer falls.

B

Boundaries

Even with a registered title the boundaries shown on the filed plan are general boundaries and are not definitive. The rule is generally what has been there for the last 12 years is the boundary this may have to be supported by statutory declarations.

Breach of a Restrictive Covenant

Or other defect.

Indemnity insurance might be available

Bridging Finance

This might be for a deposit which is repaid on the sale of the property. It is rare for English banks to extend finance for a property that is open ended. It is usually only extended once contracts are exchange and there is a fixed date for completion.

Building Regulation Consent

This may be required even if there are not developments that require planning permission. It relates to health and safety matters and the type of materials used on completion of building works for which consent it required a final certificate must be obtained from the local authority. This is evidence that the building regulations have been complied with.

C

Capital Gains Tax

The main exemption which affects residential conveyancing is the principal private dwelling house exemption The seller must have occupied the dwelling house as his only or main residence throughout the period of ownership There is a sliding scale for absences and exemptions of short periods of absence

Capacity

The seller might be sole owner, joint owner, personal representative mortgagee, charity, company bankrupt or otherwise incapacitated.

Classes of Title

There are different classes of title the best being absolute title but there is also possessory title qualified title and good leasehold title

Contaminated Land

Any contamination could have serious effects in that it may be impossible to sell or obtain a mortgage on.

Completion

The day on which the transaction is finalised, the money changes hands and the parties vacate and take possession of the land that is the moving day.

Co-Ownership

This is where more than one person owns the land such as tenant in common or joint tenant.

Conveyancing

The process of transferring the ownership of freehold and leasehold land.

Compulsory Registration

This has arisen since 1990 and applies to the whole of England and Wales. The categories of events triggering a registration have changed but it is still not compulsory to register land without one of these triggers but voluntary registration could take place.

Conservation Area

Any non listed building in a conservation area must not be demolished with conservation area consent. There are also restrictions on development.

Contract Races

This is where more than one contract has been issued solicitors are obliged to let both parties know the terms of the race that is what needs to be done to secure the property. It must be confirmed in writing. A standard contact race would specific that the first person to be in a position to exchange contracts unconditionally wins the race. This is usually signified by the purchasers solicitors producing a signed contract and deposit together with authority to proceed.

Covenants

This is a promise made in a deed and binding any subsequent owner of the land they may include such matter as maintaining the fences and only using the land for the erection of one property.

D

Deeds

Apart from unregistered land most deeds have now dematerialised as they are registered at the land registry. Evidence of ownership is shown by official copies of the registered entries. This is an official dated document showing the current state of the title.

Deposit

Although not a legal requirement is it customary and it's a form of security and part payment towards the purchase price.

Discharge of seller's mortgage

On completion is the seller has a mortgage this will need to be paid off and evidence given to the purchasers solicitor. This will need to be lodged at the land registry as proof of the discharge before a new purchaser can be substituted and maybe a new mortgage started.

Draft contract

The name attached to the contract before it is agreed by the parties and prior to exchange of contracts. Once the contract is approved it can be signed by the parties and forms the basis of the transactions. They must be in the same format. Identical contracts are exchanged.

E

Easements

This is a right over land of another such as a right of way or of light.

Engrossment

Merely means s properly types up version of a document the draft is amended then the engrossment is the fair copy

Escrow

A document such as contract mortgage transfer is delivered and will not become effective until some future date. It is therefore held in escrow the condition being that the event takes place such as completion or exchange of contracts. Gets rid of the need for all the parties to a transaction being in the same room at the same time.

Exchange of contracts

When the parties agree to bind themselves legally to buy and sell the land.

Execution

Means the signing of a document in a certain way for a deed to be valid it must contain the words this deed signed by the necessary parties in the presence of a witness and be delivered.

F

Filed plan

In conveyancing a plan is a map showing the land referred to edged in red. It is the official designation of the land for land registry purposes

Fixture and fittings

Now a formal part of the process in that purchasers solicitor will expect to see a completed fixtures and fittings form. It may be acceptable to apportion part of the price for fixtures and fittings and this is sometimes undertaken when the price falls on one of the bands for change in stamp duty. The list must be legitimate ad the revenue have the right to query this and levy any tax not paid

Fixtures and fittings distinction

Between objects not attached to the land are fittings and those attached are fixtures. The current fixtures and fitting list covers most eventualities but care should be taken if an offer is deemed to include items at the property they should be specifically mentioned in the

Full Survey

As the name suggests this is full survey of the property and should contain a detailed breakdown of every aspect of the property.

H

Home Buyers Valuation and Survey Report

This is a compromise between a full structural survey and valuation.

I

Insurance

The risk on the property passes when contracts are exchanged. Even thought he purchaser has not got possession. The property is usually also insured by the seller up until the date of completion. They both have an insurable risk.

Indemnity Covenants

Any owner of land will remain liable for the covenants and passes these on by way of an indemnity covenant by any incoming purchaser

Investigating Title

Once the seller has produced the contract package the purchasers solicitors investigate title. This is to ensure that the seller is the owner of the property which is the subject of the contract. Also it must not reveal any defects other than those can be rectified prior to exchange of contracts.

There may for instance be consent required from a third party such as the necessity to register the transfer of a lease and become the member of a management company.

J

Joint tenants

This is most common between husband and wife. Both own equal shares in the property if either were to die the other inherit by way of survivorship. They cannot leave their share by will to anyone else.

L

Listed Building

Where a building might be of outstanding historic or architectural important the secretary of state may list it. Any alterations to the property will require both planning permission and listed building consent.

M

Mortgage

Is where the owner of land borrows money on the security of the land Also known as a legal charge. The lender has certain statutory powers the most important being that they can sell the property in the event of the loan not being paid.

Mortgage Fraud

Normally some proof of identity is required but this has been overtaken by the money laundering rules whereby it is accepted practice that clients should produce to their solicitors all the usual forms of ID to include utility bills driving licence passport etc.

Mortgages Repayments

The main types of repayment are pension, endowment and interest only. They do not affect the conveyancing transaction but some may have slightly different procedures between the conveyancers and the lender such as notices or deposit of insurance policies.

O

Occupiers Rights

The most important is the spouse of the seller. They have a statutory right to occupy the matrimonial home. Usually an enquiry is made as to there being any other occupiers of the matrimonial home. They are then asked to sign the contract to confirm they will give vacant possession completion.

Office Copy Entries

Usually refers to the registered title but can relate to any official copy issued by the land or other registries. They are acceptable as the originals.

Overriding Interests

These are matters affecting the land which are not on the register although this is being resolved under the current land registry rules. The most important being rights of way not mentioned on the deeds local land charges squatters rights.

P

Planning - Use of the property

It should be checked that the property has permission for its current use. Any purchaser should be aware that any change of use form its current use may require planning permission. For example a residential property may not be used for the fixing and selling of cars without a change of use. Any breach will be enforced by the local planning authority.

Planning Breach

This could be rectified by retrospective permission or again by indemnity insurance.

Purchase Deed

Now the transfer or TR1 this is the document that is signed by the seller transferring the land from the seller to the purchaser. It is signed prior to completion and once the formalities have been finalised such as the passing of the money it will be forwarded to the purchasers solicitors. This document will need to be stamped and registered at the land registry.

Possessory Title

The registry may grant a possessory title in the event of lack of paper title and eventually it can be upgraded to an absolute title. Land can be acquired through adverse possession but it is still subject to all covenants and easements etc existing at the date of the registration

Post Contact Stage

Between exchange of contracts and completion essential things such as finance is resolved as our final searches and all documents signed in readiness for completion.

R

Radon

If the property is in an area affected by radon gas a specific search should be undertaken which will reveal whether a survey has been undertaken and remedial measures have been taken.

Registered land

A state run system that proves the ownership of land by have a title registered at the HM land registry.

S

Searches

There are a series of searches. Before exchange of contracts the local authority search, after exchange bankruptcy and land registry searches.

Special Conditions

Any special condition will be used to vary the standard conditions of sale contained in the contract

Subject to Contract

This is of historical interest now as it is not possible to exchange contracts inadvertently or entering into irrevocably buying land without a proper contract. Some organisations still insist on using it as it gives them comfort Not now necessary in view of the Law Of Property (Miscellaneous) Provisions act 1989

Survey

There are many kinds of survey form the mere valuation by a lender to a full structural survey. Any purchaser should be aware that at the moment the law says *caveat emptor* that is let the buyer beware. Apart form a deliberate misstatement the seller is not liable for the current state of the property. An invariable practice is for purchasers to be advised to have a survey of the property and not to rely solely on the building society valuation.

Title

Either the registered or unregistered proof of the seller's ownership of the land.

Title Number

Every piece of registered land has a unique title number and must be used in all official documents searches etc.

Tenants in Common

Is where two or more people own land jointly in separate shares. Either owner can pass their share by will to anyone they wish.

Tenure

The legal term for how the land is being held being either freehold or leasehold.

U

Unregistered Land

The seller has to prove title by a series of documents such as conveyances, mortgagees etc now being replaced by registered conveyancing.

Undertakings

These are promises by solicitor to undertake certain acts. The most common being that the sellers solicitor will discharge the existing mortgage. Failure to comply with the undertaking is a professional offence so therefore they will not be entered into lightly and can be relied up They should always be confirmed in writing and their terms made certain.

Upgrading Title

Either on application or on the initiative of the registrar a title may be upgraded such as possessory to absolute and the same for qualified and good leasehold title

V

Valuation

Can either be an estate agents valuation which is a financial matter for the purchasers and sellers a lenders valuation is the figure that is used to calculate how much the lender is prepared to lend. This is based on a valuers report prepared for the lender once the buyer has requested a loan. It is an assessment of the value not a survey of the property. Lenders will normally exclude liability for any defects in the property. They are not undertaking that the property is fit for its purpose just because they are prepared to lend on it.

Value Added Tax – VAT

Is payable on solicitors costs but not o the purchase price of second hand properties. There is not VAT payable on stamp duty or land registry fees in a domestic transaction.

W

Witnesses

Must be a responsible adult and is usually independent of the parties who must add name, address and occupation

STANDARD LETTERS

SALE 0F PROPERTY
First Letter to Purchaser's Solicitors

3 November, 2013

Address

Dear Sirs

Re   Property:
      Your Client:
      Our Client:

We understand that you act on behalf of ??????? of ???????????? in connection with their proposed purchase of the above from our clients ?????????????.

We would be obliged if you could confirm that if your clients have a property to sell a purchaser has been found and if your client should require finance this has been approved at least in principle.

Subject to the above being confirmed we will arrange for a draft Contract to be issued to you as soon as possible.

Yours faithfully

Letter to Building Society / Bank Requesting Title Deeds

3 November, 2013

Address

Dear Sirs

Re   Property:
       Account Number:
       Borrower:

We act for the above named clients in connection with the sale of the above property and we shall be obliged if you would please send us have the Title Deeds relating to this property.

We undertake to hold them to your order pending redemption of the mortgage.

At the same time please let us know the amount owing under this mortgage.

Yours faithfully

Authority to Bank to Obtain Title Deeds

3 November, 2013

Address

Dear Sirs

We hereby give you authority to release the Title Deeds for property listed below to …………….. of …………….

Address of Property: ……………………………………

Address of Lender: ……………………………………

Account Number: ……………………………………

Signature   ……………………………………

Letter Issuing Contract etc to Purchaser's Solicitors

3 November, 2013

Address

Dear Sirs

Re   Property:
Your Client:
Our Client:

Thank you for your letter of ????????. We take this opportunity of enclosing:

1. Draft Contract in duplicate

2. Official Copy of Register Entries plus File Plan

3. Fixtures Fittings and Contents List

4. Seller's Property Information Form

5. Copy Transfer dated ??????????

Yours faithfully

Letter Sending Approved TR1 and Replies to Requisitions on Title

3 November, 2013

Address

Dear Sirs

Re   Property:
Your Client:
Our Client:

Thank you for your letter of .... we take this opportunity of enclosing the following:

1. TR1 approved as amended

2. Requisitions on Title and our replies thereto

Yours faithfully

Letter to Purchaser's Solicitor on Exchange of Contracts

3 November, 2013
Fax & Post
Fax Number:

Address

Dear Sirs

Re   Property:
Your Client:
Our Client:

Further to our telephone conversation at 2:15 p.m. between ……
and ……… …… Contracts were exchanged and the date fixed for
completion is …………...

The sale price is £……. and you will be holding the £…….. deposit
strictly to our order pending completion.

We enclose our client's part of the Contract to complete exchange of
Contracts. .

Yours faithfully

Letter to Bank/Building Society Requesting Redemption Figure

3 November, 2013

Building Society
Address

Dear Sirs

Re: **Borrower:**
       Property:
       Account No:

Would you please let us have the redemption figure on the above mortgage account as at *date........*

Yours faithfully

Index

****

Appendix 1 Sample conveyancing costs 2 bed freehold House

PURCHASE STATEMENT FEBRUARY 2013 FOR FREEHOLD HOUSE	Using Licensed conveyancers.		
Our fees for	£ (net)	£ (VAT)	£ (Gross)
Purchase Conveyance	349.00	69.80	418.80
Preparation of the Stamp Duty Land	85.00	17.00	102.00
Transaction Return			
Money Laundering check (per customer	17.00	3.40	20.40
Professional Fee-Access online searches and Land Registry documentation	39.69	7.94	47.63
Local Search	125.00	25.00	150.00
Drainage Search	41.32	8.26	49.58
Environment Search	45.80	9.16	54,96
Bankruptcy Search	2.50	0.50	3.00
Land Registry Priority Search	4.50	0.90	5.40

Preparation of the Chancel Repair Indemnity Insurance*	17.00	3.40	20.40
Archive of documents associated with your purchase**	25.00	5.00	30.00
Total	751.81	150.36	902.17

Based on the information we have at present, the following fees may also be applicable on your transaction.

Our fees for	£ (net)	£ (VAT)	£ (Gross)
Acting for your lender for each Mortgage***(payable by you in accordance with your mortgage conditions)	150.00	30.00	180.00
Each electronic payment by CHAPS	40.00	8.00	48.00
Each electronic payment by BACS	8.50	1.70	10.20
Payments to third parties, including Government Agencies			
H.M. Land Registry charges			70.00
Government Stamp Duty			0.00
Chancel Repair Liability Indemnity Premium (inc of insurance premium tax) *			5.25
total			313.45
Overall Total			1,215,62

If there is an existing Home Information Pack with acceptable searches the Local Search Fee and Drainage Search Fee will not apply.

For other locality searches that may be required, e. g. coal search or tin search see our menu of additional services.

If the property is Leasehold, there will be additional third party payments.

- Subject to change if the purchase property cannot be covered by the Block Chancel Repair Indemnity Policy proposed. Please refer to Fact Sheet enclosed for those exceptions. If the property is an excepted case a policy may still be obtainable and we will contact you during the transaction if this is the case.

- There will be no further charge if you require retrieval of your documents in the future. Please note the charge is £25.00 plus VAT for a single transaction. A combined fee of £30.00 plus VAT will be charged for this service if a related transaction is instructed.*** If a second mortgage, other charge or secured loan is to be taken out on the property, an additional legal fee for acting for your lender plus VAT will be payable for each additional one.

Appendix 2

SCHEDULE OF DOCUMENTS TO BE USED IN CONVEYANCING

1) PROTOCOL FORMS

   a) Fixtures, Fittings and Contents (4th Edition)

   b) Sellers Property Information Form (4th Edition)

   c) Sellers Leasehold Information Form (3rd Edition)

2) General Leasehold Enquiries

3) Land Registry Forms (see overleaf for samples of these forms)

   a) SIM

   b) OC1

   c) D1

   d) TR1

   e) TP1

   f) OS1

   g) OS2

   h) DL

   i) FR1

j)   AP1

4)   Various Search Forms

   a)   Local Authority Search LLC1

   b)   Standard Enquiries for Local Authority (2002 edition)

5)   Stamp Duty Land Tax – Land transaction return (SDLT1) and Self Certificate SDLT60

6)   Completion Information and Requisitions on Title

7)   Draft contract

Land Registry
Application for an official search of the index map

If you need more room than is provided for in a panel, and your software allows, you can expand any panel in the form. Alternatively use continuation sheet CS and attach it to this form.

Land Registry is unable to give legal advice but our website www.landregistry.gov.uk provides guidance on Land Registry applications. This includes public guides and practice guides (aimed at conveyancers) that can also be obtained from any Land Registry office.

See www.landregistry.gov.uk/contact-us/offices if you are unsure which Land Registry office to send this application to.

LAND REGISTRY USE ONLY
Record of fees paid
Particulars of under/over payments
Reference number Fees debited £

Where there is more than one local authority serving an area, enter the one to which council tax or business rates are normally paid.

If no postal address insert description, for example 'land adjoining 2 Acacia Avenue'.

1	Local authority serving the property:

2	Property to be searched
	Flat/unit number:
	Postal number or description:
	Name of road:
	Name of locality:
	Town:
	Postcode:
	Ordnance Survey map reference (if known):
	Known title number:

3	Application and fee

Application	Fee paid (£)
Search of the index map	

See fees calculator at www.landregistry.gov.uk/professional/fees/fees-calculator

Place 'X' in the appropriate box.

The fee will be charged to the account specified in panel 4.

Fee payment method

☐ cheque made payable to 'Land Registry'

☐ Land Registry credit account

☐ direct debit, under an agreement with Land Registry

4	This application is sent to Land Registry by
	Key number (if applicable):
	Name: Address or UK DX box number:
	Email address: Reference:
	Phone no: / Fax no:

5 Issue of certificate of result of search in paper format where an email address has been supplied

If you have supplied an email address in panel 4, then, unless you complete the box below, any certificate of result of search of the index map will be issued electronically to that address, if there is a direction under section 100(4) of the Land Registration Act 2002 by the registrar covering such issuing.

☐ I have supplied an email address but require the certificate of result of search to be issued in paper format instead of being issued electronically

6 I apply for an official search of the index map in respect of the land referred to in panel 2 shown   on the attached plan

7

Signature of applicant: --

Date:

WARNING

If you dishonestly enter information or make a statement that you know is, or might be, untrue or misleading, and intend by doing so to make a gain for yourself or another person, or to cause loss or the risk of loss to another person, you may commit the offence of fraud under section 1 of the Fraud Act 2006, the maximum penalty for which is 10 years' imprisonment or an unlimited fine, or both.

Failure to complete this form with proper care may result in a loss of protection under the Land Registration Act 2002 if, as a result, a mistake is made in the register.

Under section 66 of the Land Registration Act 2002 most documents (including this form) kept by the registrar relating to an application to the registrar or referred to in the register are open to public inspection and copying. If you believe a document contains prejudicial information, you may apply for that part of the document to be made exempt using Form EX1, under rule 136 of the Land Registration Rules 2003.

Land Registry
Application for official copies of register/
plan or certificate in Form CI

Use one form per title.

If you need more room than is provided for in a panel, and your software allows, you can expand any panel in the form. Alternatively use continuation sheet CS and attach it to this form.

Land Registry is unable to give legal advice but our website www.landregistry.gov.uk provides guidance on Land Registry applications. This includes public guides and practice guides (aimed at conveyancers) that can also be obtained from any Land Registry office.

See www.landregistry.gov.uk/contact-us/offices if you are unsure which Land Registry office to send this application to.

LAND REGISTRY USE ONLY
Record of fees paid
Particulars of under/over payments
Reference number
Fees debited £

Where there is more than one local authority serving an area, enter the one to which council tax or business rates are normally paid.

Use a separate form for each registered title.

Place 'X' in the appropriate box.

1   Local authority serving the property:

2   Details of estate

     (a) Title number if known:

     (b) (Where the title number is unknown) this application relates to

     ☐ freehold   ☐ leasehold   ☐ manor

     ☐ franchise   ☐ caution against first registration

     ☐ rentcharge   ☐ profit a prendre in gross

3   Property

     Flat/unit number:

     Postal number or description:

     Name of road:

     Name of locality:

     Town:

     Postcode:

4	Application and fee		
	Application	Total number of all copies or certificates requested in panel 7	Fee paid (£)
	Official copy of register /plan or certificate of inspection of title plan		

See fees calculator at www.landregistry.gov.uk/professional /fees/fees-calculator

Fee payment method

Place 'X' in the appropriate box.

The fee will be charged to the account specified in panel 5.

☐ cheque made payable to 'Land Registry'

☐ Land Registry credit account

☐ direct debit, under an agreement with Land Registry

5	This application is sent to Land Registry by

If you are paying by credit account or direct debit, this will be the account charged.

Key number (if applicable):

Name:
Address or UK DX box number:

Email address:
Reference:

Phone no: Fax no:

Please note that the facility of issuing copies electronically is not available at present. When it is, a direction will appear on our website and details will be given in Public Guide 1 and Practice Guide 11. Until there is a direction, you do not need to complete this panel to obtain an official copy in paper format.

Official copies issued electronically are in 'Portable Document Format' (PDF) which replicates the appearance of the hard copy version. You will need Adobe Acrobat Reader (which you can install free from www.adobe.com) to open the document.

Place 'X' in the box if applicable.

6	Issue of official copies in paper format where an email address has been supplied

If you have supplied an email address in panel 5, then, unless you complete the box below, any official copy will be issued electronically to that address, if there is a direction under section 100(4) of the Land Registration Act 2002 by the registrar covering such issuing.

☐ I have supplied an email address but require the official copy(ies) to be issued in paper format instead of being issued electronically

7	I apply for

Indicate how many copies of each are required.

____ official copy(ies) of the register of the above mentioned property

____ official copy(ies) of the title plan or caution plan of the above mentioned property

____ certificate(s) of inspection of title plan, in which case either

Place 'X' in the appropriate box.

i. ☐ an estate plan has been approved and the plot number is:

or
ii. ☐ no estate plan has been approved and a certificate is to be issued in respect of the land shown on the attached

State reference, for example 'edged red'.

plan and copy

Place 'X' in the appropriate box.	8	If an application for registration is pending against the title
		☐ I require an official copy back-dated prior to the receipt of the application
		☐ I require an official copy on completion of that application
	9	
		Signature of applicant: --
		Date:

WARNING

If you dishonestly enter information or make a statement that you know is, or might be, untrue or misleading, and intend by doing so to make a gain for yourself or another person, or to cause loss or the risk of loss to another person, you may commit the offence of fraud under section 1 of the Fraud Act 2006, the maximum penalty for which is 10 years' imprisonment or an unlimited fine, or both.

Failure to complete this form with proper care may result in a loss of protection under the Land Registration Act 2002 if, as a result, a mistake is made in the register.

Under section 66 of the Land Registration Act 2002 most documents (including this form) kept by the registrar relating to an application to the registrar or referred to in the register are open to public inspection and copying. If you believe a document contains prejudicial information, you may apply for that part of the document to be made exempt using Form EX1, under rule 136 of the Land Registration Rules 2003.

Land Registry
Disclosable overriding interests

DI

This form should be accompanied by either Form AP1 or Form FR1.

If you need more room than is provided for in a panel, and your software allows, you can expand any panel in the form. Alternatively use continuation sheet CS and attach it to this form.

Leave blank if this form accompanies an application for first registration.	**1**	Title number(s) of the property:
Insert address including postcode (if any) or other description of the property, for example 'land adjoining 2 Acacia Avenue'.	**2**	Property:
The information in panel 3 will help us if this form becomes detached. Insert the full name(s) of the applicant on Form AP1/FR1. Where a conveyancer lodges the application, this must be the name(s) of the client(s), not the conveyancer.	**3**	This form is lodged with an application in Form AP1/FR1 made by:
The registrar may enter notice of a disclosed interest in the register of title. You may use as many Forms DI as are necessary. The plan to any certified copy lease must show all colours shown on the original. Notice of lease(s) will only be cancelled on receipt of a Form CN1 with evidence of determination. If two or more leases of the same property and the same date are listed, include a number or other identifier for each lease in the first column.	**4**	List below all unregistered disclosable leases in date order, starting with the oldest. Lodge a certified copy of either the original or counterpart of each lease disclosed.

	Description of land leased	Date of lease	Term and commencement date
e.g.	*Flat 1, garage 3 and bin store*	*24.06.2008*	*5 years from 24.06.2008*

5 List below any disclosable overriding interests other than leases. Lodge any documentary evidence within the control of the applicant that identifies the interest disclosed.

For each interest disclosed in this panel:

Give a description of the interest, for example, a legal easement.

Give details of the deed or circumstance in which the interest arose.

Complete only if the interest affects part of the title. Give a brief description of the part affected, for example 'coloured brown on the attached plan'.

a.

arising by virtue of:

affects the part(s) of the registered estate as shown:

b.

arising by virtue of:

affects the part(s) of the registered estate as shown:

c.

arising by virtue of:

affects the part(s) of the registered estate as shown:

WARNING
If you dishonestly enter information or make a statement that you know is, or might be, untrue or misleading, and intend by doing so to make a gain for yourself or another person, or to cause loss or the risk of loss to another person, you may commit the offence of fraud under section 1 of the Fraud Act 2006, the maximum penalty for which is 10 years' imprisonment or an unlimited fine, or both.

Failure to complete this form with proper care may result in a loss of protection under the Land Registration Act 2002 if, as a result, a mistake is made in the register.

Under section 66 of the Land Registration Act 2002 most documents (including this form) kept by the registrar relating to an application to the registrar or referred to in the register are open to public inspection and copying. If you believe a document contains prejudicial information, you may apply for that part of the document to be made exempt using Form EX1, under rule 136 of the Land Registration Rules 2003.

Land Registry
Transfer of whole of registered title(s)

If you need more room than is provided for in a panel, and your software allows, you can expand any panel in the form. Alternatively use continuation sheet CS and attach it to this form.

Leave blank if not yet registered.	1	Title number(s) of the property:
Insert address including postcode (if any) or other description of the property, for example 'land adjoining 2 Acacia Avenue'.	2	Property:
	3	Date:
Give full name(s).	4	Transferor:
Complete as appropriate where the transferor is a company.		**For UK incorporated companies/LLPs** Registered number of company or limited liability partnership including any prefix: **For overseas companies** (a) Territory of incorporation: (b) Registered number in the United Kingdom including any prefix:
Give full name(s).	5	Transferee for entry in the register:
Complete as appropriate where the transferee is a company. Also, for an overseas company, unless an arrangement with Land Registry exists, lodge either a certificate in Form 7 in Schedule 3 to the Land Registration Rules 2003 or a certified copy of the constitution in English or Welsh, or other evidence permitted by rule 183 of the Land Registration Rules 2003.		**For UK incorporated companies/LLPs** Registered number of company or limited liability partnership including any prefix: **For overseas companies** (a) Territory of incorporation: (b) Registered number in the United Kingdom including any prefix:
Each transferee may give up to three addresses for service, one of which must be a postal address whether or not in the UK (including the postcode, if any). The others can be any combination of a postal address, a UK DX box number or an electronic address.	6	Transferee's intended address(es) for service for entry in the register:
	7	The transferor transfers the property to the transferee

	8	Consideration
Place 'X' in the appropriate box. State the currency unit if other than sterling. If none of the boxes apply, insert an appropriate memorandum in panel 11.		☐ The transferor has received from the transferee for the property the following sum (in words and figures):
		☐ The transfer is not for money or anything that has a monetary value
		☐ Insert other receipt as appropriate:

	9	The transferor transfers with
Place 'X' in any box that applies.		☐ full title guarantee
Add any modifications.		☐ limited title guarantee

	10	Declaration of trust. The transferee is more than one person and
Where the transferee is more than one person, place 'X' in the appropriate box.		☐ they are to hold the property on trust for themselves as joint tenants
		☐ they are to hold the property on trust for themselves as tenants in common in equal shares
Complete as necessary.		☐ they are to hold the property on trust:

The registrar will enter a Form A restriction in the register *unless*:
– an 'X' is placed:
  – in the first box, or
  – in the third box and the details of the trust or of the trust instrument show that the transferees are to hold the property on trust for themselves alone as joint tenants, *or*
– it is clear from completion of a form JO lodged with this application that the transferees are to hold the property on trust for themselves alone as joint tenants.

Please refer to Land Registry's Public Guide 18 – *Joint property ownership* and Practice Guide 24 – *Private trusts of land* for further guidance. These guides are available on our website www.landregistry.gov.uk

	11	Additional provisions
Insert here any required or permitted statement, certificate or application and any agreed covenants, declarations and so on.		

The transferor must execute this transfer as a deed using the space opposite. If there is more than one transferor, all must execute. Forms of execution are given in Schedule 9 to the Land Registration Rules 2003. If the transfer contains transferee's covenants or declarations or contains an application by the transferee (such as for a restriction), it must also be executed by the transferee.

If there is more than one transferee and panel 10 has been completed, each transferee may also execute this transfer to comply with the requirements in section 53(1)(b) of the Law of Property Act 1925 relating to the declaration of a trust of land. Please refer to Land Registry's Public Guide 18 – Joint property ownership and Practice Guide 24 – Private trusts of land for further guidance.

12	Execution

Land Registry
Transfer of part of registered title(s)

If you need more room than is provided for in a panel, and your software allows, you can expand any panel in the form. Alternatively use continuation sheet CS and attach it to this form.

Leave blank if not yet registered.	1	Title number(s) out of which the property is transferred:
When application for registration is made these title number(s) should be entered in panel 2 of Form AP1.	2	Other title number(s) against which matters contained in this transfer are to be registered or noted. if any:
Insert address, including postcode (if any), or other description of the property transferred. Any physical exclusions, such as mines and minerals, should be defined.	3	Property:

Place 'X' in the appropriate box and complete the statement.

For example 'edged red'.

The property is identified

☐ on the attached plan and shown:

For example 'edged and numbered 1 in blue'.

Any plan lodged must be signed by the transferor.

☐ on the title plan(s) of the above titles and shown:

	4	Date:
Give full name(s).	5	Transferor:

Complete as appropriate where the transferor is a company.

For UK incorporated companies/LLPs
Registered number of company or limited liability partnership including any prefix:

For overseas companies
(a) Territory of incorporation:

(b) Registered number in the United Kingdom including any prefix:

Give full name(s).	6	Transferee for entry in the register:

For UK incorporated companies/LLPs
Registered number of company or limited liability partnership including any prefix:

Complete as appropriate where the transferee is a company. Also, for an overseas company, unless an arrangement with Land Registry exists, lodge either a certificate in Form 7 in Schedule 3 to the Land Registration Rules 2003 or a certified copy of the constitution in English or Welsh, or other evidence permitted by rule 183 of the Land Registration Rules 2003.

For overseas companies
(a) Territory of incorporation:

(b) Registered number in the United Kingdom including any prefix:

Each transferee may give up to three addresses for service, one of which must be a postal address whether or not in the UK (including the postcode, if any). The others can be any combination of a postal address, a UK DX box number or an electronic address.	7	Transferee's intended address(es) for service for entry in the register:

	8	The transferor transfers the property to the transferee

Place 'X' in the appropriate box. State the currency unit if other than sterling. If none of the boxes apply, insert an appropriate memorandum in panel 12.

9 Consideration

☐ The transferor has received from the transferee for the property the following sum (in words and figures):

☐ The transfer is not for money or anything that has a monetary value

☐ Insert other receipt as appropriate:

Place 'X' in any box that applies.

Add any modifications.

10 The transferor transfers with

☐ full title guarantee

☐ limited title guarantee

Where the transferee is more than one person, place 'X' in the appropriate box.

11 Declaration of trust. The transferee is more than one person and

☐ they are to hold the property on trust for themselves as joint tenants

☐ they are to hold the property on trust for themselves as tenants in common in equal shares

Complete as necessary.

☐ they are to hold the property on trust:

The registrar will enter a Form A restriction in the register *unless*:
– an 'X' is placed:
  – in the first box, or
  – in the third box and the details of the trust or of the trust instrument show that the transferees are to hold the property on trust for themselves alone as joint tenants, *or*
– it is clear from completion of a form JO lodged with this application that the transferees are to hold the property on trust for themselves alone as joint tenants.

Please refer to Land Registry's Public Guide *18 – Joint property ownership* and Practice Guide *24 – Private trusts of land* for further guidance. These guides are available on our website www.landregistry.gov.uk

Use this panel for:
– definitions of terms not defined above
– rights granted or reserved
– restrictive covenants
– other covenants
– agreements and declarations
– any required or permitted statements
– other agreed provisions.

12 Additional provisions

Definitions

The prescribed subheadings may be added to, amended, repositioned or omitted.

Any other land affected by rights granted or reserved or by restrictive covenants should be defined by reference to a plan.

Any other land affected should be defined by reference to a plan and the title numbers referred to in panel 2.

Rights granted for the benefit of the property

Any other land affected should be defined by reference to a plan and the title numbers referred to in panel 2.

Rights reserved for the benefit of other land

Include words of covenant.

Restrictive covenants by the transferee

Include words of covenant.

Restrictive covenants by the transferor

Insert here any required or permitted
statements, certificates or applications
and any agreed declarations and so on.

Other

The transferor must execute this transfer as a deed using the space opposite. If there is more than one transferor, all must execute. Forms of execution are given in Schedule 9 to the Land Registration Rules 2003. If the transfer contains transferee's covenants or declarations or contains an application by the transferee (such as for a restriction), it must also be executed by the transferee.

If there is more than one transferee and panel 11 has been completed, each transferee may also execute this transfer to comply with the requirements in section 53(1)(b) of the Law of Property Act 1925 relating to the declaration of a trust of land. Please refer to Land Registry's Public Guide *18 – Joint property ownership* and Practice Guide *24 – Private trusts of land* for further guidance.

13 Execution

Land Registry

Application by purchaser for official
search with priority of the whole of the
land in a registered title or a pending first
registration application

OS1

Use one form per title.

If you need more room than is provided for in a panel, and your software allows, you can expand any panel in the form. Alternatively use continuation sheet CS and attach it to this form.

Land Registry is unable to give legal advice but our website www.landregistry.gov.uk provides guidance on Land Registry applications. This includes public guides and practice guides (aimed at conveyancers) that can also be obtained from any Land Registry office.

See www.landregistry.gov.uk/contact-us/offices if you are unsure which Land Registry office to send this application to.

Conveyancer is a term used in this form. It is defined in rule 217A, Land Registration Rules 2003 and includes persons authorised under the Legal Services Act 2007 to provide reserved legal services relating to land registration and includes solicitors and licensed conveyancers.

LAND REGISTRY USE ONLY Record of fees paid
Particulars of under/over payments
Reference number Fees debited £

Where there is more than one local authority serving an area, enter the one to which council tax or business rates are normally paid.	1	Local authority serving the property:
Enter the title number of the registered estate or that allotted to the pending first registration.	2	Title number of the property:
Insert address including postcode (if any) or other description of the property, for example 'land adjoining 2 Acacia Avenue'.	3	Property:
Enter the full names. If there are more than two persons, enter the first two only.	4	Registered proprietor/Applicant for first registration SURNAME/COMPANY NAME: FORENAME(S): SURNAME/COMPANY NAME: FORENAME(S):

	5	Application and fee

Application	Fee paid (£)
Official search of whole with priority	

See fees calculator at www.landregistry.gov.uk/professional/fees/fees-calculator

Fee payment method

Place 'X' in the appropriate box.

The fee will be charged to the account specified in panel 6.

☐ cheque made payable to 'Land Registry'

☐ Land Registry credit account

☐ direct debit, under an agreement with Land Registry

If you are paying by credit account or direct debit, this will be the account charged.	**6** This application is sent to Land Registry by Key number (if applicable): Name: Address or UK DX box number: Email address Reference Phone no: Fax no:
Place 'X' in one box only. For a search of a registered title enter a date falling within the definition of 'search from date' in rule 131 of the Land Registration Rules 2003. If the date entered is not such a date the application may be rejected.	**7** Application and search from date ☐ I apply for a search of the individual register of a registered title to ascertain whether any adverse entry has been made in the register or day list since [ ] ☐ I apply for a search in relation to a pending application for first registration to ascertain whether any adverse entry has been made in the day list since the date of the pending first registration application.
Provide the full name(s) of each purchaser or lessee or chargee.	**8** The applicant:
Place 'X' in the appropriate box.	**9** Reason for application I certify that the applicant intends to ☐ **P**urchase ☐ take a **L**ease ☐ take a registered **C**harge
If a conveyancer is acting for the applicant, that conveyancer must sign. If no conveyancer is acting, the applicant (if more than one person then each) must sign.	**10** Signature of applicant or their conveyancer: ------------------------------------ Date:

WARNING
If you dishonestly enter information or make a statement that you know is, or might be, untrue or misleading, and intend by doing so to make a gain for yourself or another person, or to cause loss or the risk of loss to another person, you may commit the offence of fraud under section 1 of the Fraud Act 2006, the maximum penalty for which is 10 years' imprisonment or an unlimited fine, or both.

Failure to complete this form with proper care may result in a loss of protection under the Land Registration Act 2002 if, as a result, a mistake is made in the register.

Under section 66 of the Land Registration Act 2002 most documents (including this form) kept by the registrar relating to an application to the registrar or referred to in the register are open to public inspection and copying. If you believe a document contains prejudicial information, you may apply for that part of the document to be made exempt using Form EX1, under rule 136 of the Land Registration Rules 2003.

© Crown copyright (ref: LR/HO) 10/12

Land Registry

Application by purchaser for official search with priority of part of the land in a registered title or a pending first registration application

OS2

Use one form per title.

If you need more room than is provided for in a panel, and your software allows, you can expand any panel in the form. Alternatively use continuation sheet CS and attach it to this form.

Land Registry is unable to give legal advice but our website www.landregistry.gov.uk provides guidance on Land Registry applications. This includes public guides and practice guides (aimed at conveyancers) that can also be obtained from any Land Registry office.

See www.landregistry.gov.uk/contact-us/offices if you are unsure which Land Registry office to send this application to.

Conveyancer is a term used in this form. It is defined in rule 217A, Land Registration Rules 2003 and includes persons authorised under the Legal Services Act 2007 to provide reserved legal services relating to land registration and includes solicitors and licensed conveyancers.

LAND REGISTRY USE ONLY
Record of fees paid
Particulars of under/over payments
Reference number Fees debited £

Where there is more than one local authority serving an area, enter the one to which council tax or business rates are normally paid.

1 Local authority serving the property:

Enter the title number of the registered estate or that allotted to the pending first registration.

2 Title number:

Enter the full names. If there are more than two persons, enter the first two only.

3 Registered proprietor/Applicant for first registration

SURNAME/COMPANY NAME:

FORENAME(S):

SURNAME/COMPANY NAME:

FORENAME(S):

4 Application and fee

Application	Fee paid (£)
Official search of part with priority	

Fee payment method

See fees calculator at www.landregistry.gov.uk/professional/fees/fees-calculator

Place 'X' in the appropriate box.

The fee will be charged to the account specified in panel 5.

- [ ] cheque made payable to 'Land Registry'
- [ ] Land Registry credit account
- [ ] direct debit, under an agreement with Land Registry

	5	This application is sent to Land Registry by

If you are paying by credit account or direct debit, this will be the account charged.

5 This application is sent to Land Registry by

Key number (if applicable):

Name:
Address or UK DX box number:

Email address:
Reference:

Phone no:	Fax no:

Insert address including postcode (if any) or other description of the property, for example 'land adjoining 2 Acacia Avenue'.

6 Property to be searched:

(a) Where an estate plan has been approved

    (i) the plot number(s) is/are [ ]

    (ii) the date of approval of the estate plan is [ ]

    OR

A plan must be attached when (b) is completed.

(b) The property is shown [ ] on the attached plan.

    OR

Insert title number.

(c) The property is shown [ ] on the title plan of [ ]

Provide the full name(s) of each purchaser or lessee or chargee.

7 The applicant:

Place 'X' in one box only.

For a search of a registered title enter a date falling within the definition of 'search from date' in rule 131 of the Land Registration Rules 2003. If the date entered is not such a date the application may be rejected.

8 Application and search from date

[ ] I apply for a search of the individual register of a registered title to ascertain whether any adverse entry has been made in the register or day list since [ ]

[ ] I apply for a search in relation to a pending application for first registration to ascertain whether any adverse entry has been made in the day list since the date of the pending first registration application.

9 Reason for application
I certify that the applicant intends to

Place 'X' in the appropriate box.

[ ] **P**urchase

[ ] take a **L**ease

[ ] take a registered **C**harge

If a conveyancer is acting for the applicant, that conveyancer must sign. If no conveyancer is acting, the applicant (if more than one person then each) must sign.

10

Signature of applicant
or their conveyancer: _____

Date:

WARNING
If you dishonestly enter information or make a statement that you know is, or might be, untrue or misleading, and intend by doing so to make a gain for yourself or another person, or to cause loss or the risk of loss to another person, you may commit the offence of fraud under section 1 of the Fraud Act 2006, the maximum penalty for which is 10 years' imprisonment or an unlimited fine, or both.

Failure to complete this form with proper care may result in a loss of protection under the Land Registration Act 2002 if, as a result, a mistake is made in the register.

Land Registry
List of documents

— Please complete and lodge this form in duplicate.
— If the application is a first registration application and you supply the original and a certified copy of a statutory declaration, stamp duty land tax certificate, subsisting lease, subsisting charge or the latest document of title (for example any conveyance to the applicant) we will return the original; if a certified copy is not supplied, we may retain the original document and it may be destroyed.
— If the application is not a first registration application and you supply a certified copy of an original document we will return the original; if a certified copy is not supplied, we may retain the original document and it may be destroyed.

1	Property address including postcode (if any):

2 Documents lodged with this form
— The first column is for Land Registry use only. If Land Registry places an asterisk '*' in this column, it shows that we have kept that document.
— Please number the documents in sequence; copies should also be numbered and listed as separate documents.
— You need not list the names on land charges searches. Simply enter the search number.

Land Registry use only	Item no	Date	Document type	Parties

Land Registry use only	Item no	Date	Document type	Parties

Land Registry
Application for first registration

You must lodge the documents of title with this application; these must be listed on Form DL.

If you need more room than is provided for in a panel, and your software allows, you can expand any panel in the form. Alternatively use continuation sheet CS and attach it to this form.

Land Registry is unable to give legal advice but our website www.landregistry.gov.uk provides guidance on Land Registry applications. This includes public guides and practice guides (aimed at conveyancers) that can also be obtained from any Land Registry office.

See www.landregistry.gov.uk/contact-us/offices if you are unsure which Land Registry office to send this application to.

Conveyancer is a term used in this form. It is defined in rule 217A, Land Registration Rules 2003 and includes persons authorised under the Legal Services Act 2007 to provide reserved legal services relating to land registration and includes solicitors and licensed conveyancers.

	LAND REGISTRY USE ONLY Record of fees paid
	Particulars of under/over payments
	Reference number Fees debited £

Where there is more than one local authority serving an area, enter the one to which council tax or business rates are normally paid.

1 Local authority serving the property:

Insert address including postcode (if any) or other description of the property, for example 'land adjoining 2 Acacia Avenue'.

On registering a rentcharge, profit a prendre in gross or franchise, insert a description, for example 'Rentcharge (or as appropriate) over 2 Acacia Avenue'.

2 Property:

Place 'X' in the appropriate box. Only use the third option where the property has an address and is fenced on the ground.

Enter reference, for example 'edged red'.

Enter nature and date of document.

3 The extent of the land to be registered can be clearly identified on the current edition of the Ordnance Survey map from

☐ the attached plan and shown:

☐ the plan attached to the:

☐ the address shown in panel 2

Place 'X' in the appropriate box.

4 The class of title applied for is

☐ absolute leasehold
☐ absolute freehold
☐ good leasehold
☐ possessory freehold
☐ possessory leasehold

5 Application, priority and fees

Applications in priority order	Price paid/Value (£)	Fees paid (£)
First registration of the freehold/leasehold estate		
Total fees (£)		

See fees calculator at www.landregistry.gov.uk/professional/fees/fees-calculator

Fee payment method

☐ cheque made payable to 'Land Registry'

☐ direct debit, under an agreement with Land Registry

Place 'X' in the appropriate box.

The fee will be charged to the account specified in panel 7.

Provide the full name(s) of the person(s) applying for first registration. Where a conveyancer lodges the application, this must be the name(s) of the client(s), not the conveyancer.	6	The applicant:
Complete as appropriate where the applicant is a company. Also, for an overseas company, unless an arrangement with Land Registry exists, lodge either a certificate in Form 7 in Schedule 3 to the Land Registration Rules 2003 or a certified copy of the constitution in English or Welsh, or other evidence permitted by rule 183 of the Land Registration Rules 2003.		**For UK incorporated companies/LLPs** Registered number of company or limited liability partnership including any prefix: **For overseas companies** (a) Territory of incorporation: (b) Registered number in the United Kingdom including any prefix:

	7	This application is sent to Land Registry by
If you are paying by direct debit, this will be the account charged.		Key number (if applicable):
This is the address to which we will normally send requisitions and return documents. However if you insert an email address, we will use this whenever possible.		Name: Address or UK DX box number: Email address: Reference:
		Phone no: · · · · · · · · · · · · · · · · Fax no:

Place 'X' in the appropriate box.	8	The address(es) for service for each proprietor of the estate to be entered in the register is
In this and panel 10, each proprietor may give up to three addresses for service, one of which must be a postal address whether or not in the UK (including the postcode, if any). The others can be any combination of a postal address, a UK DX box number or an electronic address.		☐ the address of the property (where this is a single postal address) ☐ the following address(es):

Where the applicant is more than one person, place 'X' in the appropriate box.	9	Where the applicant is more than one person
		☐ they hold the property on trust for themselves as joint tenants
		☐ they hold the property on trust for themselves as tenants in common in equal shares
Complete as necessary.		☐ they hold the property on trust:
The registrar will enter a Form A restriction in the register *unless*: – an 'X' is placed: – in the first box, or – in the third box and the details of the trust or of the trust instrument show that the applicants are to hold the property on trust for themselves alone as joint tenants, *or* – it is clear from completion of a form JO lodged with this application that the applicants are to hold the property on trust for themselves alone as joint tenants.		
Please refer to Land Registry's Public Guide *18 – Joint property ownership* and Practice Guide *24 – Private trusts of land* for further guidance. These guides are available on our website www.landregistry.gov.uk		

10	Name and address(es) for service for the proprietor of any charge to be entered in the register:

For UK incorporated companies/LLPs
Registered number of company or limited liability partnership including any prefix:

For overseas companies
(a) Territory of incorporation:

(b) Registered number in the United Kingdom including any prefix:

11 Disclosable overriding interests

☐ Disclosable overriding interests affect the estate.

12 Certificate

The title is based on the title documents listed in Form DL which are all those under the control of the applicant.

Details of rights, interests and claims affecting the estate (other than non-disclosable interests falling within rule 28(2) of the Land Registration Rules 2003) known to the applicant are, where applicable, disclosed in the title documents and Form DI if accompanying this application.

☐ The applicant knows of no other such rights, interests and claims. Only the applicant is in actual possession of the property or in receipt of the rent and profits from the property.

☐ The applicant knows only of the following additional such rights, interests and claims, including those of any person (other than the applicant) in actual possession of the property or in receipt of the rent and profits from the property:

13 Examination of title

☐ I/we have not fully examined the applicant's title to the estate, including any appurtenant rights, or satisfied myself/ourselves that it has been fully examined by a conveyancer in the usual way prior to this application.

14 Confirmation of identity

When registering transfers, charges, leases and other dispositions of land, Land Registry relies on the steps that conveyancers take, where appropriate, to verify the identity of their clients. These checks reduce the risk of property fraud.

Full details of the evidence of identity that is required can be found in Practice Guide 67 and in Public Guide 20.

Where a person was not represented by a conveyancer, Land Registry requires 'evidence of identity' in respect of that person, except where the first alternative in panel 15(2) applies.

'Evidence of identity' is evidence provided in accordance with any current direction made by the Chief Land Registrar under section 100(4) of the Land Registration Act 2002 for the purpose of confirming a person's identity.

The requirement of registration is contained in section 4, Land Registration Act 2002. Further guidance is contained in Practice Guide 1.

If this application is to register a transfer, lease or charge, dated on or after 10 November 2008 **and** the requirement of registration applies, complete one of the following

Place 'X' in the appropriate box.

Conveyancer is defined in rule 217A, Land Registration Rules 2003 and includes persons authorised under the Legal Services Act 2007 to provide reserved legal services relating to land registration and includes solicitors and licensed conveyancers.

☐ I am a conveyancer, and I have completed panel 15

☐ I am not a conveyancer, and I have completed panel 16

15 Where the application is sent to Land Registry by a conveyancer

(1) Details of conveyancer acting

If you are sending an application to register a transfer, lease or charge, for each party to each disposition that is to be registered, state in the table below the details of the conveyancer (if any) who represented them.

Where a party is not represented by a conveyancer you must also complete (2) below.

Place 'X' in the box in the second column if the person or firm who is sending the application to Land Registry represented that party in the transaction. Otherwise complete the details in the third column. If the party is not represented insert 'none' in the third column.

Name of transferor, landlord, transferee, tenant, borrower or lender		Conveyancer's name, address and reference
	☐	Reference:
	☐	Reference:
	☐	Reference:

(2) Evidence of identity

Where any transferor, landlord, transferee, tenant, borrower or lender listed in (1) was not represented by a conveyancer

Place 'X' in the appropriate box(es).

Insert the name of each unrepresented transferor, landlord, transferee, tenant, borrower or lender for whom you give this confirmation.

☐ I confirm that I am satisfied that sufficient steps have been taken to verify the identity of

and that they are the transferor, landlord, transferee, tenant, borrower or lender listed in (1) (as appropriate)

Evidence of identity is defined in panel 14. Full details of the evidence of identity that is required can be found in Practice Guide 67.

☐ I enclose evidence of identity in respect of each unrepresented transferor, landlord, transferee, tenant, borrower or lender for whom I have not provided the confirmation above

16 Where the application is sent to Land Registry by someone who is not a conveyancer

(1) Details of conveyancer acting

If you are sending an application to register a transfer, lease or charge (ie a mortgage), for each party to each disposition that is to be registered, state in the table below the details of the conveyancer (if any) who represented them.

You must also complete (2) below.

If the party is not represented insert 'none' in the second column.

Name of transferor, landlord, transferee, tenant, borrower or lender	Conveyancer's name, address and reference
	Reference:
	Reference:
	Reference:

(2) Evidence of identity

Place 'X' in the appropriate box(es).

☐ for each applicant named in panel 6 is enclosed

Evidence of identity is defined in panel 14. Full details of the evidence of identity that is required can be found in Public Guide 20.

☐ for each unrepresented transferor, landlord, transferee, tenant, borrower or lender listed in (1) is enclosed

If a conveyancer is acting for the applicant, that conveyancer must sign.

17

Signature of conveyancer: _____

Date:

OR

If no conveyancer is acting, the applicant (and if the applicant is more than one person then each of them) must sign.

Signature of applicant: _____

Date:

Land Registry
Application to change the register

If you need more room than is provided for in a panel, and your software allows, you can expand any panel in the form. Alternatively use continuation sheet CS and attach it to this form.

Land Registry is unable to give legal advice but our website www.landregistry.gov.uk provides guidance on Land Registry applications. This includes public guides and practice guides (aimed at conveyancers) that can also be obtained from any Land Registry office.

See www.landregistry.gov.uk/contact-us/offices if you are unsure which Land Registry office to send this application to.

Conveyancer is a term used in this form. It is defined in rule 217A, Land Registration Rules 2003 and includes persons authorised under the Legal Services Act 2007 to provide reserved legal services relating to land registration and includes solicitors and licensed conveyancers.

LAND REGISTRY USE ONLY
Record of fees paid
Particulars of under/over payments
Reference number Fees debited £

Where there is more than one local authority serving an area, enter the one to which council tax or business rates are normally paid.

1 Local authority serving the property:

Full postcode of property (if any):

Enter the title number of each title that requires an entry to be made in that register.

2 Title number(s) of the property:

Place 'X' in the appropriate box.

Give a brief description of the part affected, for example 'edged red on the plan to the transfer dated ....'.

3 The application affects

☐ the whole of the title(s)

☐ part of the title(s) as shown:

See fees calculator at www.landregistry.gov.uk/professional /fees/fees-calculator

4 Application, priority and fees

Applications in priority order	Price paid/Value (£)	Fees paid (£)
	Total fees (£)	

Fee payment method

Place 'X' in the appropriate box.

The fee will be charged to the account specified in panel 7.

☐ cheque made payable to 'Land Registry'

☐ direct debit, under an agreement with Land Registry

List the documents lodged with this form. Copy documents should be listed separately. If you supply a certified copy of an original document we will return the original; if a certified copy is not supplied, we may retain the original document and it may be destroyed.	**5** Documents lodged with this form:
Provide the full name(s) of the person(s) applying to change the register. Where a conveyancer lodges the application, this must be the name(s) of the client(s), not the conveyancer. Complete as appropriate where the applicant is a company. Also, for an overseas company, unless an arrangement with Land Registry exists, lodge either a certificate in Form 7 in Schedule 3 to the Land Registration Rules 2003 or a certified copy of the constitution in English or Welsh, or other evidence permitted by rule 183 of the Land Registration Rules 2003.	**6** The applicant: For UK incorporated companies/LLPs Registered number of company or limited liability partnership including any prefix: For overseas companies (a) Territory of incorporation: (b) Registered number in the United Kingdom including any prefix:
If you are paying by direct debit, this will be the account charged. This is the address to which we will normally send requisitions and return documents. However if you insert an email address, we will use this whenever possible.	**7** This application is sent to Land Registry by Key number (if applicable): Name: Address or UK DX box number: Email address: Reference: Phone no: Fax no:
Complete this panel if you want us to notify someone else that we have completed this application.	**8** Third party notification Name: Address or UK DX box number: Email address: Reference:
Place 'X' in the appropriate box. In this and panel 10, each proprietor may give up to three addresses for service, one of which must be a postal address whether or not in the UK (including the postcode, if any). The others can be any combination of a postal address, a UK DX box number or an electronic address.	**9** The address(es) for service for each proprietor of the registered estate(s) to be entered in the register is ☐ the address of the property (where this is a single postal address) ☐ the address(es) for service from the transfer/assent ☐ (for existing proprietors who are remaining in the register) the current address(es) for service in the register ☐ the following address(es):

Where a charge has an MD reference we will ignore an address given in this panel unless the charge is in favour of a United Kingdom bank and neither the charge form nor any agreement we have with the lender specifies an address for service.

For permitted addresses see note to panel 9.

Complete as appropriate where the lender is a company. Also, for an overseas company, unless an arrangement with Land Registry exists, lodge either a certificate in Form 7 in Schedule 3 to the Land Registration Rules 2003 or a certified copy of the constitution in English or Welsh, or other evidence permitted by rule 183 of the Land Registration Rules 2003.

If this statement applies (i) place 'X' in the box and (ii) enclose Form DI.

Section 27 of the Land Registration Act 2002 lists the registrable dispositions.

Rule 57 of the Land Registration Rules 2003 sets out the disclosable overriding interests that you must tell us about.

Full details of the evidence of identity that is required can be found in Practice Guide 67 and in Public Guide 20.

Place 'X' in the appropriate box.

Conveyancer is defined in rule 217A, Land Registration Rules 2003 and includes persons authorised under the Legal Services Act 2007 to provide reserved legal services relating to land registration and includes solicitors and licensed conveyancers.

---

10   Name and address(es) for service of the proprietor of any new charge to be entered in the register:

For UK incorporated companies/LLPs
Registered number of company or limited liability partnership including any prefix:

For overseas companies
(a) Territory of incorporation:

(b) Registered number in the United Kingdom including any prefix:

---

11   Disclosable overriding interests

☐   This application relates to a registrable disposition and disclosable overriding interests affect the registered estate.

---

12   Confirmation of identity

When registering transfers, charges, leases and other dispositions of land, or giving effect to a discharge or release of a registered charge, Land Registry relies on the steps that conveyancers take, where appropriate, to verify the identity of their clients. These checks reduce the risk of property fraud.

Where a person was not represented by a conveyancer, Land Registry requires 'evidence of identity' in respect of that person, except where the first alternative in panel 13(2) applies.

'Evidence of identity' is evidence provided in accordance with any current direction made by the Chief Land Registrar under section 100(4) of the Land Registration Act 2002 for the purpose of confirming a person's identity.

If this application is to register a transfer, lease or charge, or to give effect to
a discharge in Form DS1 or a release in Form DS3 complete one of the following

☐   I am a conveyancer, and I have completed panel 13

☐   I am not a conveyancer, and I have completed panel 14

13   Where the application is sent to Land Registry by a conveyancer

(1) Details of conveyancer acting

If you are sending an application to register a transfer, lease or charge, for each party to each disposition that is to be registered state in the table below the details of the conveyancer (if any) who represented them.

Where a party is not represented by a conveyancer you must also complete (2) below.

Place 'X' in the box in the second column if the person or firm who is sending the application to Land Registry represented that party in the transaction. Otherwise complete the details in the third column. If the party is not represented insert 'none' in the third column.

Name of transferor, landlord, transferee, tenant, borrower or lender		Conveyancer's name, address and reference
	☐	
		Reference:
	☐	
		Reference:
	☐	
		Reference:

If you are sending an application to give effect to a discharge in Form DS1 or release in Form DS3 for each lender, state in the table below the details of the conveyancer (if any) who represented them.

Where a lender is not represented by a conveyancer you must also complete (2) below.

Place 'X' in the box in the second column if the person or firm who is sending the application to Land Registry represented that party in the transaction. Otherwise complete the details in the third column. If the party is not represented insert 'none' in the third column.

Name of lender		Conveyancer's name, address and reference
	☐	
		Reference:
	☐	
		Reference:

(2) Evidence of identity

Where any transferor, landlord, transferee, tenant, borrower or lender listed in (1) was not represented by a conveyancer

Place 'X' in the appropriate box(es).

Insert the name of each unrepresented transferor, landlord, transferee, tenant, borrower or lender for whom you give this confirmation.

☐ I confirm that I am satisfied that sufficient steps have been taken to verify the identity of

and that they are the registered proprietor or have the right to be registered as the registered proprietor

Evidence of identity is defined in panel 12. Full details of the evidence of identity that is required can be found in Practice Guide 67.

☐ I enclose evidence of identity in respect of each unrepresented transferor, landlord, transferee, tenant, borrower or lender for whom I have not provided the confirmation above

14 Where the application is sent to Land Registry by someone who is not a conveyancer

(1) Details of conveyancer acting

If you are sending an application to register a transfer, lease or charge (ie a mortgage), for each party to each disposition that is to be registered, state in the table below the details of the conveyancer (if any) who represented them.

You must also complete (2) below.

If the party is not represented insert 'none' in the second column.

Name of transferor, landlord, transferee, tenant, borrower or lender	Conveyancer's name, address and reference
	Reference:
	Reference:
	Reference:

If you are sending an application to give effect to a discharge in Form DS1 or release in Form DS3, for each lender state in the table below the details of the conveyancer (if any) who represented them.

You must also complete (2) below.

If the party is not represented insert 'none' in the second column.

Name of lender	Conveyancer's name, address and reference
	Reference:
	Reference:

(2) Evidence of identity

Place 'X' in the appropriate box(es).

Evidence of identity is defined in panel 12. Full details of the evidence of identity that is required can be found in Public Guide 20.

☐ for each applicant named in panel 6 is enclosed

☐ for each unrepresented transferor, landlord, transferee, tenant, borrower or lender listed in (1) is enclosed

15

If a conveyancer is acting for the applicant, that conveyancer must sign.

Signature of conveyancer: ----------------------------------

Date:

OR

If no conveyancer is acting, the applicant (and if the applicant is more than one person then each of them) must sign.

Signature of applicant: ----------------------------------

Date:

WARNING

If you dishonestly enter information or make a statement that you know is, or might be, untrue or misleading, and intend by doing so to make a gain for yourself or another person, or to cause loss or the risk of loss to another person, you may commit the offence of fraud under section 1 of the Fraud Act 2006, the maximum penalty for which is 10 years' imprisonment or an unlimited fine, or both.

Failure to complete this form with proper care may result in a loss of protection under the Land Registration Act 2002 if, as a result, a mistake is made in the register.

Under section 66 of the Land Registration Act 2002 most documents (including this form) kept by the registrar relating to an application to the registrar or referred to in the register are open to public inspection and copying. If you believe a document contains prejudicial information, you may apply for that part of the document to be made exempt using Form EX1, under rule 136 of the Land Registration Rules 2003.

© Crown copyright (ref: LR/HO) 10/12